Writing the Land:
Foodways and Social Justice

Published by NatureCulture LLC

www.nature-culture.net
www.writingtheland.org

Copyright © 2022
by
NatureCulture LLC

ISBN: 978-1-7375740-4-0

Front & Back Covers:
Seed by Martin Bridge and design by Martin Bridge
https://www.thebridgebrothers.com
Interior book design: Lis McLoughlin

Other books in this series:
Writing the Land: Windblown I (2022)
Writing the Land: Windblown II (2022)
Writing the Land: Maine (2022)
Writing the Land: Northeast (2021)

Related volume:
Honoring Nature (2021)

Series/related books publishers: 2022 NatureCulture LLC; 2021 Human
Error Publishing
For more information: www.nature-culture.net

Writing the Land:
Foodways and Social Justice

Edited by Lis McLoughlin, PhD

Published by
NatureCulture LLC
Northfield, MA

Opening Thought:
Food is Not a Thing

Food is not a thing. But our dominant culture thingifies food; it's packaged and offered to us as a thing we find in the grocery store. That's the primary way that people think about food and interact with food, on the weekly trip to the grocery store, rather than walking out your back door to see how much the spinach has grown, or putting food scraps into the soil that are going to nourish this plant that is then going to nourish you and your family. That kind of connection to food that is very material and energetic is really not there for a lot of people now. So when you talk about reproduction—reproducing— think about how the ways that food is grown also reproduces a relationship with food and a relationship with land. You grow food as a thing, then it's going to be consumed that way. And it's not reproducing this relational, "I nourish you, you nourish me" kind of reciprocal Relationship. You grow food native to the ecosystem and for a local community, then You grow relationships of interdependency.

—JuPong Lin,
(excerpt of a conversation with Hyperion Çaca Yvaire)
August 2022

Introduction
Foodways and Social Justice: Writing a Complex Web

Part I: Conserving, Restoring, and Creating Food-Producing Lands and Communities

Each chapter of Part I tells a story of a land conservation organization—-how and why they are passionate about conserving food-producing lands. Every one of these organizations goes about it slightly differently day by day on and in the ground. They all care deeply about the combined fate of humans and land: past, present, and future. Each holds a piece of the larger puzzle of how we keep agricultural land producing food sustainably, and how we interact with nature, the land, and one another fairly.

Part II: The Arts, Foodways, Communities and Conserved Lands

Part II of this book, explores the important role the arts play in embodying, communicating, and enhancing the connections among foodways, land conservation, and social justice. Each essay tells a story of an arts or agricultural organization or artist and how they contribute to this work.

Overall, there are many ways to do good work in this arena. But none of them is simple.

Every organization focuses their energy in one or more key areas depending upon the values and passions that drive them: justice, the arts, individuals, community, land, agriculture, and food production. These concepts are a tangled web that is enhanced and strengthened by the many intersections of threads that cross and recross, making a strong network.

Join us in celebrating the complexity of ways people can work together ethically, practically, and with joy and hope to conserve food-producing lands for all of nature—-ourselves included.

—L. McLoughlin, PhD, August 2022

TABLE OF CONTENTS

PART I: CONSERVING, RESTORING, AND CREATING FOOD-PRODUCING LANDS AND COMMUNITIES

continues next page......

PART I:
CONSERVING, RESTORING AND CREATING FOOD-PRODUCING LANDS AND COMMUNITIES

Photo: Open the Gate by Mary Swander

SUSTAINABLE IOWA LAND TRUST

Iowa

Our Mission:
To permanently protect Iowa land to grow nature-friendly table food.

-Red Fern Farm—Mary Swander
-Jupiter Ridge Farm—Rita Mae Reese
-Grade A Farm—Paul Brooke
-Phoenix Farm—Rebecca Wee
-Driftless Hills Farm—Dana Maya

Sustainable Iowa Land Trust
by Suzan Erem

We are SILT. We hold sand and clay together. We bind everything. From us, roots reach deep and stems reach skyward. We teem with life. We absorb energy that pours down upon us and transform it into something strong and nurturing. We know everything decays, then feeds the next.

Our founders lived through the crisis that created us. We drove by the farm gate auctions. We glanced at tears pooled in wrinkled cheeks. We watched as generations of struggle went for pennies on the dollar. We saw implements lifted from overgrown fields where they'd over-wintered for half a century.

Children were torn from the land and transplanted into concrete towns. Fathers were forced to work inside year 'round, answering to college kids half their age. Mothers scrabbled to hold families together without even a root cellar to keep them fed. Everyone woke and fell asleep with the question, "Why?" carved into their hearts with the rusty knife of debt.

We had lived by the rules and lost. We blamed ourselves for not working hard enough, not thinking smart enough, not being good enough. Desperate, not knowing what more to do, we borrowed from the wisdom of sticks. We gathered together to become unbreakable. We held tight to our truth, (when doubt didn't rule), that this wasn't our fault, this loss, this pain, this grief the media called the Farm Crisis.

Families stood side by side, bound by a nameless cruelty, braced by generations they feared they'd betrayed. It was too late. Forces they couldn't see made way for a world they couldn't imagine. Farm houses were plowed under. Farm machines grew ever larger, planting seas of fuel and feed. Schools closed. Churches shuttered. Small towns died. Weeds grew through their broken streets like worry through a broken dream.

A generation remembers the days. We asked ourselves, Is it really too late? So here we are, stirred again by tiny lives, like nematodes and fungi. We still can't know the minds of a Wells Fargo or Citibank any more than soil knows the mind of the sun. But we've learned a few things in a lifetime or two. We've witnessed a bug bring the world to its knees. We've seen derechos level a town. This is what power looks like. This is how change happens. It builds upon all that came before it and it cleans house when necessary. We build SILT upon the glacial till of the Prairie Fires, Farmers Unions, Family Farm Defenders and Farm Coalitions dying back and growing again year after year by people who cared enough to tend them for the decades we needed to evolve. We will make room on this landscape for what our future needs of us – healthy food, water, soil and each other.

Still, the wind grows strong with stench. It spins us around and blows us over with ferocity and sometimes guile. Farmers who grow food fall silently into the well-crafted crack between ag and business lenders. Organic is too high risk for the market. Food is a "specialty crop." Every farmer is a "family" farmer. Hog confinements are "barns." Water pollution is water "quality." Ball parks are named for banks, community centers for corporations. Public universities brand new buildings with company names while academic freedom wilts on the vine. And every day, thousands of acres are bought and sold, never to feel a footstep again.

SILT remains. We live by mantras such as, "Diversity builds resilience" and "All farms need wildness." We gather our microscopic forces. We honor our geological history. We spread the wealth of our energy. We support partner pollinators who give our compact strength its legs and wings. We nurture rhizomatic movements whose tendrils grow wide like strawberries yet sturdy like prairie.

We know great forces amass beyond our humble existence. They pummel us like the strengthening storms and suffocate us like a relentless drought. They are dedicated to a vision that does not even recognize us, while every day they stand upon us, harvesting our wealth.

We know they are there, and it does not matter. We are SILT. We, too, are a force of nature.

Red Fern Farm

Red Fern Farm
by Mary Swander

1.

Corn is not the answer.
Then what is?
Chestnuts planted into the rich soil
at Red Fern Farm, just two miles
from where the Mississippi River flows,
where the paleo people lived 10,000 years ago,
mammoth hunters whose points you've held in your hands,
then the archaic people struggled
with droughts and dry prairie, giving way
to the mound builders and the Oneotos,
living in pine forests along rivers and streams,
the last prehistoric culture, giving way
to the Ioway, Meskwaki, Sac and Fox,
Ho-Chunk, Black Hawk, and Sioux.
All who broke very little ground,
who kept no livestock,
who kept the earth In place
in a place where the sky was black
with migrating pelicans, ducks, and geese,
diving down to fish in the wetlands
with the turtles, frogs and snakes looking on.
It's for the birds' sake, for the sake of all
who've preserved this land,
for the sake of the native people,
the native prairie, the sake of all
the settlers and sons and daughters
of the homesteaders trying to claim
a home, trying to make a buck
on "free land," land parceled out
to anyone who could stick it out five years.
For the sake of the sons and daughters

of the sons and daughters who stayed
for generations, pushed
to expand, to do as they were told
with tillage, chemicals and yields,
trying to get big before they had to get out.
But you wouldn't be told.
And the chestnuts began to grow.

2.

And so did the heartnuts, hazelnuts, honey and
aronia berries, Asian pears, cornelian cherries,
and hardy kiwi vining up the sides of trees.
And so did the persimmons,
sweet, mild, rich and picked
in the early fall, the days still warm,
the fruit still hard, ripening off the branches,
tasting like an apricot-- maybe even better--
smelling like sweetened dough
with a dash of cinnamon.
Too soft to slice, simply cut in half,
the flesh scooped out for a smoothie,
a compote, a dried treat, a pudding
or upside down cake with the pulp mixed
with flour, baking soda, nutmeg,
cloves, chopped pecans and lemon zest.
What, no Delicious apples? No Bartlett pears?
No, nothing to be pruned.
No vegetables? No broccoli, tomatoes, sweet corn?
No, nothing to be dug up, turned over.
Only asparagus or horseradish that comes up
all on its own from year to year.
And for the future?
No annual crops.
An easement in place, protecting the farm
from the bulldozer, lapsing back into row crops,
the speculator with a housing development

or a theme park with flashing neon signs
and rides and slides shooting
screaming teens into an artificial lake.
Only perennials: drowning in trees, bushes, shrubs
that will grow well in this changing climate zone.
Who knows what the future will bring?
Thirty years from now, the persimmon
may find the weather too tough.
"Now, that's pretty extreme," the land trust had said.
"Yes, yes, that's extreme." You said.
"We are extremists."

3.

The paw-paws, too, are extremists,
extreme in their beauty, the maroon flowers
drooping down, producing a massive amount
of fruit on a single stem, the green bounty quietly
camouflaged, understated, hidden beneath its leaves,
the Quakers of the farm--like you, their owners--
mild in manner, mild in taste,
custardy like a banana crossed with mango.
Unlike apples, peaches, and pears,
the paw-paws never crossed the ocean.
A native tree familiar to the Meskwaki,
the Sac and Fox, the Ho-Chunk and Sioux.
A lucky find, a food source for the settlers.
But good for only two days,
paw-paws never hit the road,
never shipped across the country.
No one ever picked them
and put them in their pocket for long.
So the apples, peaches, pears pushed them aside,
and the paw-paws went way down yonder.
Yet here on Red Fern Farm, next to the chestnuts
and persimmons, the paw-paws bear witness,
greet Bosnians who crossed the ocean,

fleeing war, recreating their old world
custom of picking nuts in the fall.
The Bosnians pull into the u-pick farm
in their vans with buckets and baskets.
Their vehicles fill with just a little
of what they left behind.
The nut wizard whirls across the ground
beneath our feet, in this ever-shifting place,
tree roots sinking in, communicating
through an intricate web of fungi
growing around and inside them,
telling the dirt to stay put,
stopping it from washing down river,
from carrying harm,
finding no one, nothing displaced.

Photo: Pawpaw Flower at Red Fern Farm by Suzan Erem

Jupiter Ridge Farm

Poetry exists primarily in the gift economy but I have to admit I had not thought much about agriculture or land existing in much the same way, not until I visited Jupiter Ridge Farm with the intention of harvesting a poem. Meeting Will Lorentzen and Adrian White was a gift, of course, and I gave a silent thanks to poetry, which has gifted me with so many wonderful people. The connections it provides are often immediate, often enduring, and never superficial. Will showed me and my daughter around the land, and told us about the man who had built the structures, including the house, and then gave them all away, both to protect the land itself and to make farming a viable option for the next generation. After the past few years of isolation and despair, getting to witness this gift was a revelation, a reprieve, and a revival for me.

My daughter and I left Jupiter Ridge Farm with a shiitake log and a deer antler. The log is in my backyard now, and no doubt I'll have nearly forgotten it by the time it fruits into mushrooms. The antler is on my mantlepiece, daily connecting me back to land and people hundreds of miles away, and to a cycle of gifts and connection that give me hope for a livable world for our children.

—-Rita Mae Reese, June 2022

Photo: Shitake Mushrooms at Jupiter Ridge Farm by Suzan Erem

Exercises in Impermanence
by Rita Mae Reese

—for Will, Adrian and Jupiter Ridge Farm, 2022

The wind here is fierce and Will is nervous
about the trees overhead. He gives us an antler
and tells how the mice, in their endless hunger,
devour them each spring. The wind and water
and mice provide daily lessons in
impermanence. Clothes are drying

everywhere. How their fingers must have
ached from the cold. They have just replaced
the broken washing machine.
I imagine them, load after load, as the demands
of the land mount and guests—my daughter
and me—make their way toward them.

The farm is at the point where the Dakota Sioux,
Báxoje, and Illini tribes converged, if maps can be
believed, if maps can show things like people
converging. There are debts here that can't be
repaid. The ground is black where they
started small fires to keep the big fires

away. A man named Steve built the house
and the large shed himself and then
gave it all away to strangers. Will brings
us a stone hammer, round and so big I can
barely hold it with one hand, wrap my fingers
to the notches someone created in it

who knows how long ago, but certainly before
1837 when the people were all forced west.
There are countless nicks on the surface,
evidence of years of use, probably generations
of hands, generations of work. I try not to
think of its last owner leaving it behind,

of the emptiness of his hand, a stone hammer
now in his chest where he can't claw it out
and smash everything that needs to be smashed.
For 185 years the land held the hammer—
longer than most of what we consider
permanent—until Adrian spotted it,

at first mistook it for an animal skull until
she felt its weight. 185 years to pass the hammer
from one hand to another, the land holding it,
as it holds everything—our dead, our hunger,
our dreams, and our seeds. Will and Adrian honor it
with work and with a silence that is rich

like the earth where the fire has blackened it.
Devastation, yes, but beneath it hope greening still.

Photo: Jupiter Ridge View from Tractor by Suzan Erem

Grade A Farm

The Ravine
> And the Organic Farm (Part One)
>> *—a double exposure contrasting two paradigms of farming*

by Paul Brooke

Beyond timber, discarded cars smoldered.
> Today, hay softened and saved garlic.

Their bodies scattered like hidden boulders.
> Brome wandered to the edges of the crick:

Tea kettles; ice boxes; rusted mattress springs;
> Morel mushrooms; wild ginger; columbine;

Coils, coils of barbed wire; Mason Jar rings;
> Coneflowers; honeysuckle; and grape vines.

Back then, refuse was erosion control.
> Now, buffers protect plants; hands pull burrs.

Back then, fires melted tires; farms ate coal.
> Now, bundles of garlic cure from rafters.

Photo: Mice double exposure with Nash Ambassador in Ravine by Paul Brooke

The Ravine
    And the Organic Farm (Part Two)
        —*a double exposure contrasting two paradigms of farming*
by Paul Brooke

Back then. Soybeans. Corn. Cattle fattened.
    Now, sprouts started, tended, a month early.
Till. Till. Till. Soil depleted and saddened.
    Garlic sold at Farmer's Market fairly.
Hogs farrowed in filth, finished with Paylean.
    Recycled wood in the barn unconcealed.
Weeds eradicated with Atrazine.
    Laying hens rotated from field to field.
The old dictum of land was to subtract.
    New dictum is to replenish, replace.
War drove weak men to rape and to ransack.
    Listening to the land teaches pure grace.

Photo (above): Fence Post by Paul Brooke

Photo (opposite): Garlic Double Exposure on Grade A Barn
by Paul Brooke

The Ravine
     And the Organic Farm (Part Three)
          —a double exposure contrasting two paradigms of farming
by Paul Brooke

Fouled oil poured out and gas tanks left to rot.
     Fawns asleep in tall grass undisturbed.
Mud and shit stand shin deep in the feedlot.
     Bees stockpile honey unperturbed.
Soil blows from fields. Corn wastes in the silo.
     Black locusts harvested for fence posts.
Machines flatten like massive mastodons.
     Apple trees in fog are beautiful ghosts.
To love something is not subjugation.
     To love something requires long-term concern,
Not rash return, not one generation:
     Children, water, apple trees, fawns and ferns.

Photo: Fawn Double Exposure on Discarded Pump by Paul Brooke

Phoenix Farm

Begin Anywhere
by Rebecca Wee

On the unspooling pale gravel roads, then.
With last autumn's milkweed husks waving us on

to the end of Strawbridge Road. In Iowa. Begin
with Rapid Creek's crawl through this stretch

of Midwestern spring. The air sparkles
with goldfinch, sparrows, and wind. Begin then

with wind and what it carries. In the rippling
ditch-grass one tulip's red cup of light. To the left

a swath of small suns in the grass. So start
with weeds and the drift of your feet, how they

raise small clouds from the chalky road. There's no one
to greet you, just the descant of sixty-three acres

of coarse and tended pasture, trees new and seasoned,
hills stitched with itinerant fenceline. Insects so small

you won't see them. A rooster's midday alert or oblation,
then a nest of blue eggshells and open beaks

in the beams of a bridge. Begin writing them down,
don't hassle the robin or massive oak that's worn

the weather for one hundred years. Begin where you stand
unruffled, alert, in a burnished hour, with this wonder

you've come to: a bit of earth doing its thing around you.
Begin with how happy you are.

For Phoenix Farm in Four Parts
by Rebecca Wee

I. Iowa

My daughter would rather live anywhere else. She's thirteen. Born here
in a summer storm.

I watch her watching herself as we drive, impossible blue beyond her
disdain for each lavish vista and mile. I hope she'll travel far enough

to return with some love for how this place holds its own
close, how vital its landscape of fields. Despite everywhere there is to go.
Despite the reasons to leave.

Today she's focused on eyebrows. I didn't think about eyebrows, not
once, at thirteen.

But I lamented my hair to my grandmother at the ranch near Sand Lake.
She smiled from the staircase landing, lifted from her head the hair I did
not know was a wig. "What were you saying, honey? About your hair?"

We know all things and nothing at all at thirteen. At fifty-nine. Just that
more and more

is at risk. The outdoors we ran through as kids turns spidered and steep —
too hot, too blistering cold. It tangles our hair, we get grit in our shoes,
break a nail. We get no signal wherever we stand. No fashion. No merch.
Why do we live in Iowa?
 Why not Texas, New York, Hermosa Beach?
Someplace where something happens.

II. Write the Land

I drove west from Forest Road to Phoenix Farm to be a poet again,
on behalf of the land.
Not parent or teacher. Not someone folding sheets in a cluttered mess
of rooms.

The objective: to witness a tract of earth I'd not known was here
and may not visit again. To write it. Three poems. What does it mean
to live and work and raise children where nothing happens? To outlast
grief and those we love. To age

and forget what happened last week. The words *lighthouse* or *agate*.
To marry someone from lifetimes ago. To come back to this place to live.

III. Wildness

I didn't know how things worked on farms, but my mother did.
She did not romanticize much.

So bewitched and afraid of the weather and sky, as a kid I stayed inside.
Away from the hay-dust, the goats' devil eyes. Even the barn cats
couldn't be trusted. Not even the sheep. My grandmother

lost seven fingers to the pulley on a hayrack she'd climbed at five. People
drowned in silos of grain. Froze in ditches of snow miles from home.

IV. Phoenix Farm

The phoenix of Egypt was scarlet and gold and sang alone throughout
500 years. Eagle-sized, it died in a nest of spices it set aflame and flew
into. A mythical bird that worshipped the sun, it destroyed itself to be
reborn.

A new season, again and again.

Phoenix Farm is tacitly rampant with woods, canvas structures,
equipment and fields. A hammock in a bit of shade, chicks and pullets
scattering. Rolls of hay shine in the fields, blackbirds

ride updrafts like embers, a stream lazes under a bridge. My daughter
would rather be anywhere else.
There's nothing happening here.

Santos in his broad hat waves hello. He grows pawpaws and beans. An abundance of greening and brown earth blooms here. Seaberries, apples, chestnuts and pears. He feeds people who don't know him or what he does; how he works this earth, preserves the land. The sun is intense. He feeds us from this place. I see his blackened round of a cookfire. Wave back.

if we dream it
by Rebecca Wee

in the dream we have nonstop deja vu
all through the opaque dark. a white
tarp barn lifts from the ground, then
settles itself— a bingo tent for the barred
owls and turkeys running the show.
an almost-cyclone contained. for now.

so we breathe surrounded by UFOs
caught in the fenceline. we stay silver
all night under the stars, green and
lush day by quiet day. it's taken forever
to land here. to pick off the charred feathers,
remove our masks. hang Christmas lights.
to notice the dust on the mud makes silt
good for crops.

in the dream a phoenix grimy with ash
struggles in the fire pit while blue jays
and chickadees sing from the sky. like
angels or poems or drones. then from
the road a convoy of noise we've always
known – armor and swords. elections

and weapons and playground fights.
no wonder we hide or flee. no wonder
we don't sleep. it's 2022 a.m. and we don't
know where our children are. we're told
that the slender trees along the creek are
wrapped in plastic to discourage the deer.

in the dream the five grounded clouds
are grazing sheep we've not noticed before.
dysfunctional deja vu. should we count
our blessings or the woollen sheep following
each other back to the barn? Santos waves
again from a ridge as the damp robin nestlings
in the bridge's ribs keep pecking through
their blue shells.

Photo: Guests walk back from visiting the orchard at Phoenix Farm by
Suzan Erem

Driftless Hills Farm

Understory
by Dana Maya

We've come far, from our city to this farm & been
invited to the back porch, to talk with the grownups
The husband tells us how long the winter was,
how he drove 167 miles to sell carrots & eggs &
lamb & pork to the city people who would pay. *He's tired.*
His wife tells us. They aren't sure about the yield
or the crops or whether they can weather next season

Almost out of sight, the understory:
below the picnic table, their two children, 4 & 6 years old
have built a world: their animals, a stuffed black & white kitten,
red fox, white dog & others are busy selling & serving
at a market-stand. Tiny piles of leaves of grass are laid out
on chips of bark, glass jars filled with pink flower petals.
Speckled rocks clink into glasses *would you like ice, ma'am?*
for the thirsty clientele. *And an omelet for you?*

Whatever reckonings continue above,
below, in this shade, a bounty is growing. There's no
stopping it. A steady line of hungry customers files in. Each
approaches & chooses bowl after plate of rich rock, dark dirt,
& tender shoots. One after another, each one leaves
satisfied, *yes, thank you,* full, *yes,* glad.

Photo: Understory Market by Dana Maya

Witness
by Dana Maya

Oaks & cottonwoods
alfalfa fields, nettle, milkweed,
dogbane, scrawny apple seedlings,
a fox's skull

the land remembers the forest that came before

empty pig pens, hollow hoop houses
the skeletons of farm machines

(some dreams are perennials, passed on—
others are left behind, still others
are starters—experiments in generation)

a sudden downpour, then
light, air, & sun mix to make
an ordinary glory: *Rainbow!*

the arc a massive bloom,
shooting from soil to sky. It
compels us off the porch to stand

in the field & point: how many before
us stood this same ground
to see this sudden harvest?

Tender
by Dana Maya

Tender as in one who cares
for the pigs, the sheep, & the delicate eggs,

Tender as in how to touch
chamomile, peppermint, nettles, alfalfa,
soft skin of strawberries

Tender as in the word for payment asked &
payment offered. Each open hand, receiving.

Tender is soil & sell, culture & coin.
Farm keepers, food eaters:
Keep tending, keep tending, keep
tending.

Photo: Tender Shoots by Dana Maya

DOWNEAST SALMON FEDERATION

 Maine

Downeast Salmon Federation (DSF)'s mission is to conserve wild Atlantic salmon, other sea-run fish and their habitats, restore a viable recreational salmon fishery, and protect other important river, scenic, recreational, and ecological resources in eastern Maine.

Downeast Salmon Federation's land trust supports our mission by conserving over 6,100 acres of riparian habitat, vernal pools, wetlands and salt marsh. DSF has permanently protected over 45 miles of river and stream where the last of America's endangered Atlantic salmon and other sea-run fish still breed.

-Pleasant River Community Forest—Rodger Martin and Linda Warren
-Sprague's Falls Preserve—Suzanne S. Rancourt

Essayist: Haley Stein

Downeast Salmon Federation: Working Towards a Future for Wild Fish in Maine
by Haley Stein

Downeast Maine, known for blueberries and fresh lobster, created an ecosystem around their harvest. Downeasters build their lives around these foods, the products of industries responsible for such milestones as buying a house or putting kids through college. These foods can be a lifeline for keeping Maine's rural towns in motion. River fisheries once held this status for the people of Maine. For certain species of fish like alewives, smelt, and eels, they still do, to some extent.

Mainers depending on its harvest will face challenges in the future, as warmer waters suggest a lobster migration to the north. As with the story of the lucrative sardine industry, which boomed in the region during the 19th and early 20th centuries, only to fall drastically to overfishing—the people and economy of Downeast Maine will likely have to find new avenues to provide for themselves and their families. Downeast Salmon Federation (DSF) seeks to return rivers and river fish to their important role in sustaining our communities.

Before colonization and the industrialization that followed in this region, indigenous peoples e.g. the Penobscot and the Passamaquoddy depended on river fish, not only as food, but as sustenance. As tribal member Edward Bassett writes "Water and fish are sacred to the Passamaquoddy [...] deeply embedded into our history, culture, traditional beliefs and legends and spirituality." (Bassett, Edward. "Cultural Importance of River Herring to the Passamaquoddy People," Sipayik Environmental Department, Pleasant Point Reservation, Passamaquoddy Tribe. 9-5-14 (amended 2-11-15). Page 2)

By bringing back endangered Atlantic salmon and other river fish, we bring back the connection between people and landscape, a kind of dignity that comes with harvesting your own food, and a oneness that only exists if the landscape is healthy.

DSF has witnessed and been a part of a restored heritage fishery. Removing the dam on the Pleasant River in 1989 resulted in a productive smelt population and a restored fishery. Every year since, DSF holds a

Smelt Fry in March, ringing in the smelt run and celebrating their return to Maine rivers.

Bringing people together to eat fish from their own rivers, creates a reason for folks to care about the now lesser-known species that were once such an integral part of Maine's heritage.

Similarly, the alewife, a river herring historically eaten and used as a baitfish, faced such dramatic population decline in Maine's waterways that people forgot they even could be smoked, served and eaten. At the turn of the century, alewife numbers reached historic lows due to pollution, unsustainable fishing practices, and dams. Serving as food for ocean fish, the species that prey on alewife also saw decline in numbers over those years.

Alongside other local organizations, DSF advocated for investments in river connectivity: removing dams and building fishways. Our research monitoring the alewife has proved the success of conservation practices that promote fish passage. In under 20 years, alewife populations in Downeast Maine have gone from near nonexistence to abundance, with rivers tinted black from the density of the fish in the spring season.

We celebrate the alewife run in festivals like Alewife Days, held annually in late May with local collaborators the Greenhorns just like we do for the smelt run in March. In addition to feeding folks over Alewife Days, we teach curious and willing festival-goers how to catch the river herring themselves using a dip net.

Inviting community members to interact with the fish in their rivers creates a new relationship to the tradition of wild fish harvest in Maine, visualizing a success in habitat conservation and opening a conversation about long-term environmental change.

And while we cannot yet enjoy Atlantic salmon together, as people of Maine did before its endangered status listing, we can show our community what other bounty is available to them today if basic principles of conservation are applied to rehabilitating our rivers, and help them envision a future where the same is possible for the delicacy of wild Atlantic salmon.

Applying conservation practices as a means to restore salmon and other sea-run fish habitat requires that we look beyond river water quality and flow, to the land that surrounds the rivers. DSF Land Trust acquires and maintains land riparian habitats, conserving the areas as easements. We work with local landowners, the state, and other agencies who want to see the wild forests and rivers of Maine thrive. Many DSF properties allow responsible logging, hunting, fishing, and swimming onsite. We want public access to be upheld forever: the land DSF protects cannot be developed.

In addition to the Land Trust, DSF operates two state-of-the-art salmon hatcheries. Raising wild salmon in hatcheries, DSF further modernizes the approach to conservation. Like agriculture on land, Mainers are now taking to aquaculture to grow fish and seaweeds as consumer goods. Aquaculture is one of Maine's fastest growing industries, but unlike other operations in the area that raise fish in pens specifically to be bought and sold by grocery stores, restaurants, and direct consumers, DSF applies aquaculture practices towards stocking Maine rivers with native species.

Our ultimate goal is to remove the need for our hatcheries, to stock enough Atlantic salmon that they can maintain their populations productively in their own right. Since 1947, Atlantic salmon fishing has been illegal due to their protected status. Our vision is a return to a recreational heritage fishery of Atlantic salmon, one informed by sustainability, and established enough for Maine people to catch and eat wild Maine fish.

Maine is the last holdout for Atlantic salmon in the USA. Our vision is an abundance of fish to the point of feeding Maine families, and a recreational fishery that can further connect people to this place and to the long lineage of Maine's heritage fishing. One day we hope to, once again, share meals with Mainers where wild Atlantic salmon is a mainstay on the dinner plate. And in this process, we offer a new perspective around a responsible harvest, so that Mainers can enjoy heritage fishery into the future.

Photo (opposite): Alewives in a Traditional Smokehouse
by Haley Stein

Pleasant River Community Forest

Poets Linda Warren and Rodger Martin found inspiration at the Pleasant River Community Forest in Columbia Falls. With 391 acres and a mile and a half frontage on the Pleasant River, this is a preserve for all seasons. The loop trails at Pleasant River Preserve offer hiking, snowshoeing and cross country skiing adventures. The campsite near the river is a great spot to hike into for a picnic and swim, or for a weekend adventure.

Three Rivers
by Rodger Martin

Capped in white, an eagle pair soar
with a juvenile over the tidal kirk
that is the East Machias River.
Their constant Kyries a supplication
to a dream, a belief, that what has
been done, can be undone
were we as constant as the eagle.
Along the Pleasant, a beaver sculpts
the trunk of an oak to a spindle
leaving the tree upright, balanced,
like a ball on the nose of a seal
who awaits the perfect moment
to bring it down.
A rowboat is beached nearby
along the quiet flats of the Otter,
even were it Michaelangelo sitting with his oars,
he would know we exceeded our limits
and his Pietà now would be
upstream, at the falls of the Otter,
where salmon once leapt with the eels.

Pleasant River
by Linda Warren

Gnawed down, wasp-waisted, two and a half foot trunk
on a six inch pedestal.

Our guide has a bet with a colleague over when it will fall.
Not where. Beavers know their business; it will fall in the river.

There it will lie, disrupting the current,
and the beavers will feed on its twigs at their leisure.

Elvers in the spring will navigate around it
as they migrate upstream to spawn.

A big trout will lurk beneath the trunk,
trout memory whispering him to wait
for nymphs drifting with the current,
elvers swimming against it.

On this protected bend of river
the land and water have dominion.

I will bring my grandson here,
when he is angry and afraid
in the turbulent wake of his parents' divorce.

Here, no human will disrupt the flow.

Sprague's Falls Preserve

*Poet Suzanne S. Rancourt explored DSF's Spragues Falls Preserve in Cherryfield
and stayed at the Boar's Nest there. Sprague's Falls is a hide-away where the artists
who created Bambi gained inspiration. This preserve has 608 acres of land protected
along 5.5 miles of river with trails, a wonderful swimming hole, a historic camp, and
an abandoned homestead to explore. The 1930's era Boar's Nest log cabin is chained
to several trees on the bend of the Narraguagus River to keep it from floating away
when the water is high!*

Dorothy's Silent Hiking Boots
by Suzanne S. Rancourt

The only place I have to be is here
The only person I have to be is here
The only thing I have to do is hear

Photo: Otter Falls by Chistopher Canipe

At what point is a human parasite too much for even the natural world to
recover? (asking for a friend)
by Suzanne S. Rancourt

into deep forests this west river pushes me
wind skims its surface into aged flesh.
tobacco into smoke
the trees ask
how can they trust again after so many false promises?

how does the healing take shape
sitting in red windsor chairs among lanterns with globes
encapsulating dragonfly carcasses?
what does this new healing look like
after sleep after resting

from hands that poured subsistence decades ago
kerosine congealed with age
what promises were made and broken
hearth is heart - stubborn determination equates caring with
we haven't forgotten

keep the fire going
remember relationship
dragonflies' glass shard wings- mirror fragments -
reflect September sunsets
for grandchildren to hear how the mosquito sings

Photo: A wild salmon (left) swims alongside a DSF hatchery salmon (right, clipped fin). Photo by Mitch Monini

PECONIC LAND TRUST

PECONIC LAND TRUST

New York

Founded in 1983 by a small group of local residents, Peconic Land Trust conserves Long Island's working farms, natural lands and heritage for our communities now and in the future.

-Quail Hill Farm—Scott Chaskey

Peconic Land Trust

Peconic Land Trust works with landowners, community groups, partner organizations, donors, and government at all levels to conserve Long Island's agricultural, natural, and cultural resources for all to enjoy and experience. What does this mean:

Fresh local food * Clean drinking water * Healthy water for swimming, kayaking, fishing and shellfishing * Vibrant habitats for plants, birds, and animals * Hiking trails and vistas that enrich the body, mind and soul . . . and so much more!

For the Trust, *working farms* is an important aspect of our work – in addition to conserving farmland we support the livelihood of farming on Long Island. Through our Farms for the Future Initiative, we are helping new farmers get established as they enter the field. We are working with both new and established farmers to acquire (lease or purchase) agricultural land; providing access to grants and capital improvement programs that assist with equipment and infrastructure improvements and purchases; and providing educational programs, including a well-established apprenticeship program in community supported agriculture (CSA) at our Quail Hill Farm.

Quail Hill Farm

On land donated to the Peconic Land Trust by Deborah Ann Light, Quail Hill Farm in Amagansett, New York is one of the original Community Supported Agriculture (CSA) farms in the U.S.

Since it was established in 1990, Quail Hill Farm has grown to 35 acres feeding over 500 families. The community farm also delivers fresh food to local restaurants and food pantries, and participates at local farmers' markets throughout the season.

A central part of our mission at Quail Hill is to educate the community on issues such as soil health, biodiversity, food access and local food systems, and regenerative farming practices.

Creating climate resilience for our communities is an important focus of our work – by preserving land along shorelines we are providing buffers for storm surge; by working with our local agricultural partners we are ensuring that farmland is available to farmers growing food and giving them the tools and resources to care for the land and water. Protecting the land that sits above Long Island's sole source aquifer provides a critical component to ensuring that our drinking water has the space to recharge; and protecting land adjacent to our waterways helps to buffer contaminants from entering our bays, ponds, tributaries, ocean, and sound.

Please enjoy a poem by Scott Chaskey, our original Quail Hill farmer about the farm.....and plan a visit to one of our many conserved properties on Long Island.

Laird at the Croft
by Scott Chaskey

As rough stone
sharpens steel
a man walks

under the hill,
through wet grasses
to tilled field.

Hoe in hand,
hand to wood,
layers of loam sing

rain, sun, leaves
woven with weed—
red root, purslane, lamb's quarters—

and ocean's strong song.
Tool of conduct: hoe.
Hickory shaft

caked with soil
and cool tendrils.
Work. Breathe. Sharpen steel.

Feel this stone
ground to loam
with glacial water.

Woven in grass and silt
a fertile, earthen
intelligence.

Photos: Quail Hill Farm courtesy of Peconic Land Trust

AGRARIAN TRUST

AGRARIAN TRUST

Nationwide

During the next two decades, it's estimated that more than 400 million acres and $1.4 trillion of farmland will change ownership. Agrarian Trust's mission is to support access to land for the next generation of farmers. Toward this end, Agrarian Trust supports existing Agrarian Commons 501(c)(2) land holding entities, while expanding the Agrarian Commons model across the U.S., enabling communities to hold equity and authority, create shared ecological stewardship, and support land access for diversified, regenerative agriculture. We see this model as a necessary and innovative approach to address the realities of farmland owner demographics, wealth disparity, farm viability, and all who are excluded and marginalized from equity in land, food, and community.

-West Virginia Agrarian Commons:
  New Roots Farm, Fayetteville, WV—Amy M. Alvarez
-Middle Tennessee Agrarian Commons:
  Long Hungry Creek Farm, Red Boiling Springs, TN—Julie Sumner
-Meadowlark Hearth Organic Farm:
  Scottsbluff, NE—Duane L. Herrmann
-Central Virginia Agrarian Commons:
  Callie Walker Farm, Petersburg, VA—Leona Sevick
-Puget Sound Agrarian Commons:
  Black Seed Agroecology Farm & Village, Bayview, WA—Catalina Cantú

Agrarian Trust

In the United States and around the world, skyrocketing land prices, growing inequality, and a rapidly degrading environment are threatening the ability of farmers and their communities to access land, and produce nutritious, affordable food. Agrarian Trust is pioneering a new model of land ownership, tenure, and equity—the Agrarian Commons—as a direct response to this crisis.

By removing land from the marketplace and placing it in the control of local communities and their farmers, the Agrarian Commons model ensures that farmers have affordable, long term, and secure access and tenure to land. Commonly held land also has the potential to form the basis of a revived agrarian culture, in which diverse communities are free to develop meaningful, durable relationships with their shared environments.

At the center of this approach is a renewed emphasis on the commons and communal land ownership as the future of land stewardship.

For the past 400 years, land that has traditionally been held in common has been stolen, fenced off, and ruthlessly exploited for the benefit of a small number of colonial settlers. Even early conservation efforts, purportedly founded to protect Nature, were based on the violent displacement of Indigenous people and the enforcement of conservation easements that were created without the consent or input of those who lived on and benefited from the land.

As a result, building a commons that is based on local community control is a critical step towards dismantling the racist, settler colonial system of land tenure on which US agriculture is built.

Expanding the Agrarian Commons also means unbinding the concept of "community" to include non-human partners as agents of change and mutual responsibility. Soil, water, plants, birds, and other wildlife co-mingle with humans in Agrarian Commons leases as fellow commoners, whose needs are understood as closely intertwined with the needs of the human community.

Featured Agrarian Commons

West Virginia Agrarian Commons/ New Roots Community Farm

The West Virginia Agrarian Commons is a statewide project, founded by New Roots Community Farm and community supporters. This Agrarian Commons is committed to shifting agricultural land out of the commercial real estate market and ensuring its perpetual stewardship by West Virginia farmers, with the belief that decommodifying land can be an antidote to the extractive industries that have ravaged the state over two centuries.

Located in the southern part of the state, New Roots Community Farm is a diversified, women-led farm that has grown with community support and regenerative practices. In order to promote a more just and sustainable form of economic development, New Roots serves as a local food aggregation and distribution site, offers affordable leases to farmers, runs a demonstration farm for intensive vegetable production, and provides a variety of training and educational opportunities.

Middle Tennessee Agrarian Commons/ Long Hungry Creek Farm

Middle Tennessee Agrarian Commons is a collective of organic and CSA farms creating legacy and cultivating food, culture, and agrarian connections to the Nashville foodshed and the Middle Tennessee region. This region encompasses counties that are among both the ten wealthiest and the ten poorest in the country.

Long Hungry Creek Farm is one of the oldest organic farms and CSA's in the country. Under the stewardship of Jeff Poppen, also known as "the Barefoot Farmer," Long Hungry Creek Farm provides around 150 farm shares to members in the Nashville area. Home to a thriving apprenticeship program, the farm has inspired countless young farmers to pursue a life of care for the land and service to the community.

Meadowlark Hearth Organic Farm

Meadowlark Hearth Organic Farm is a 492 acre organic farm in Scottsbluff, Nebraska. Primarily a seed farm, Meadowlark Hearth Organic Farm is located 4,000 feet above sea level on the Ogallala Aquifer. Since they founded Turtle Tree Biodynamic Seed Initiative in 1994, Farmers Nathan and Beth Corymb have been leaders in biodynamic seed production. Now, Nathan and Beth are working with Agrarian Trust to permanently conserve their land for community based, regenerative agriculture in the form of a new Agrarian Commons.

Central Virginia Agrarian Commons/ Callie Walker Land

The BIPOC-led Central Virginia Agrarian Commons supports control of land for building resilient regional food systems. Central Virginia Agrarian Commons currently seeding relationships, partnerships, and collaborations that will result in our holding urban and rural farmland to address food production and aggregation/distribution needs of Black, Indigenous, and other farmers of color in the region.

The Callie Walker Land was recently donated by methodist preacher Callie Walker, and will be the future home of the first production farm in the Central Virginia Agrarian Commons.

Puget Sound Agrarian Commons/ Black Seed Agroecological Farm and Villages

The Puget Sound Agrarian Commons began with a ten-acre farmland gift on Whidbey Island, and exists to advance food sovereignty and farmland viability in Washington State. In the context of escalating land prices in the region and historically rooted structural barriers to BIPOC land tenure, the Puget Sound Agrarian Commons acts to represent and resource Indigenous and POC collective stewardship goals and land tenure security.

Black Seed Agroecology Farm & Village is the first farm to join the Puget Sound Agrarian Commons. Black Seed is a project of Modest Family Solutions, and grows food to gift and sell to BIPOC communities, facilitates youth agroecology education, and helps to establish economic stability and a dignified food supply chain.

Photo (top): New Roots Community Farm by Agrarian Trust
Photo (bottom) New Roots Community Farm by Braiden Maddox

New Roots Community Farm

Four Postcards from New Roots Farm
by Amy M. Alvarez

To get to the farm, I drove across New River Gorge Bridge—one of the highest bridges in the country spanning one of the oldest rivers in the world. The bridge was built the year you were born and two years before my parents met. That is, the bridge is and is not that old on a human scale. The badly named New River has seen it all—retreat of glaciers, the Shawnee forcibly removed, partition of West Virginia from its eastern neighbor, birth of hellbenders. I stopped at the abandoned house on the road leading to the farm. Its ghost stood in patient lace at the window.

***

Two young white women farmers, Kate and Flannery (the latter an English major, of course), walked with me through drifts of shin-high snow toward greenhouses they built with local lumber and circular saws the year before. The greenhouses were limned with tiny lettuces, arugula, abundant rows of spinach and kale. All summer in a humid plastic hut. They showed me the rows of garlic they'd planted in the fall. Kate leapt on seeing the green scapes just breaking through the surface, coffee nearly spilling from her mug. The sky was empty. Everything was written on our hands.

***

The earth gives up its warmth, but the wind is still ice. I walked down the hill toward the pond and geese through fields that are fallow, except for the parts a local farmer uses for hay. A century ago, this land was breeding ground for pit ponies. The ponies lived in the coal mines and were hoisted above ground in summer. When the mines shut down, farmers raised cattle and pigs. Kate says that if you don't make hay, brambles grow in the fields. Just like you, land drifts back to a self-protecting wildness.

***

After a morning at the farm, I hiked down and back up the Kaymoor Miners Trail. I slid over slick stone. A falling icicle nearly got me as I took a picture of the waterfall. Under rhododendron leaves, I thought of Carter G. Woodson at seventeen reading newspapers to Black miners shrouded in black coal dust in return for ice cream and tea. At the entrance of the mine, a sign remains: YOUR FAMILY WANTS YOU TO WORK SAFELY. There are 764 steps to Kaymoor Bottom. The mine shaft is now filled and fitted with iron bars. I think you might like it here—the mosses, the shadows, the elevation gained and lost.

Long Hungry Creek Farm

*These poems are inspired by Long Hungry Creek Farm, which is located near
Red Boiling Springs, Tennessee. I learned a great deal about biodynamic farming
from farmer, Jeff Poppen, who began using this farming method in the 1970s and
is considered by many younger generations of farmers as the father of biodynamic
farming in the Southeast. He now he consults with organic farms all over the region
and goes by the moniker of "The Barefoot Farmer." You can find him on YouTube
as well. He's basically brought the philosophies and practice of German writer and
scientist Rudolph Steiner back to life here in Tennessee. He's translated Steiner's
works on agriculture, and restored a kind of knowledge I think a lot of us have lost:
knowledge about planting with the seasons, using herbal preparations, crop rotation,
maintaining cows for the right manure. The farm becomes one integrated organism
with these practices. Steiner's theories are the inspiration for the second poem in this set.
This philosophy also plays into the second poem about a daikon radish. The daikon
radish is really kind of a cover crop planted in the fall and winter in fallow ground
to restore nutrients to the earth when they're plowed under. But they also make great
pickles!*

—Julie Sumner, May 2022

Photo: Long Hungry Creek Farm by Alan Messer

Daikon
by Julie Sumner

Mild and cool as spring water,
the flesh of this radish on
my tongue. I sliced and salted it,
plunged it into the brine.

I set the pickles in the relish
dish of my mother's mother,
a clear, glass boat floating
on the sea of Thanksgiving's

table, pickles I made just
for an old friend, homesick
for his Korea this year.
His face becomes childlike

as he tastes the pickled daikon,
taste the most delicious path
back to a once-loved place,
and he asks me *Where*

*in Tennessee did this
daikon come from?* Sweetness
of the pickle still in my own
mouth like fresh-cut hay,

I say, remembering the sun,
the cocoa-powdered earth,
the parade of kale and collards,
Long Hungry Creek Farm.

November, Long Hungry Creek Farm
by Julie Sumner

As the sun plunges through
a vortex of clouds, the blue
autumn sky becomes a canvas
for the light, for the wind,

for the air itself as it brushes
over the strands and stalks
of sunflower skeletons, the air
itself a messenger of distant

galaxies, of nitrogen and carbon,
of water and dust and pollen,
all manner of stories and song
sent earthward from the moon,

the stars, each oak tree translating,
each pea shoot and radish leaf
transmuting the language of life
that rings through this whole

grand universe to the silent earth,
shifting its fine silica as an ear,
as a mother who in leans closer
to her child in order to hear.

Broken Ground
by Julie Sumner

Backbreaking the spring,
rows of seedlings, sewn one
after the other and the other,
straight lines gathering earth
like pleats on a woman's skirt,

heartbreaking the way the soft,
warm air draws the sap upward
through the greening leaves
of the young spinach just as it does
for the horseweed, the creeping thistle.

Photo: Long Hungry Creek Farm by Agrarian Trust

Meadowlark Hearth Organic Farm

Action Acts On
by Duane L. Herrmann

Government knife cuts up
the family farm:
small slice with house,
barns and gardens,
the balance over there –
hundred acre fields,
pastures, ponds.
Separating them all –
major four-lane highway.
This is the story
in rural America when
farmer has no voice
despite
owners for generations
and feeding the world.

"Give first importance
to agriculture,
tilling of the soil."*

* paraphrase of Bahá'í scripture

Meadowlark Hearth
by Duane L. Herrmann

I. Tiny Lives

Rows of tiny babies
reaching for light,
for life, for love –
love from sun above,
which, with water,
gives them life.
Garbed in green
and green remains
until maturity when
buds burst forth
into blossoms and
glory is revealed.
Divine growth process
and fruit of the plant
begins to appear
concealing, nurturing
seeds for next life
which cycles on.

II. This One Place

Under cottonwoods, tall,
gnarled, stately guardians,
through bushes out
flat to the river,
also flat, meandering
wide and slow,
one feels steady,
constant pace this land
of sand. These trees
for centuries have
watched humans pass –

one civilization after
another, marking the land
its own.
Currents change again
eschewing chemical promise
to more natural ways,
old and proven,
combining from
wisdom once dismissed
but proved needful
and essential.
Farm takes new form, while
chickens roam in colors,
and cows low
as wind blows
through trees, branches, grasses.

III.   Seeds of Life

Seeds are the germ,
the life behind
humans and their many
civilizations
from time before.
Seeds carry the past
into futures.
Meadowlark Hearth
Farm preserves,
renews seeds
to carry on, trusting
future times to be –
a venture of hope preserving
precious vintage seeds
year to year renewing
life to continue –
Seeds.
It's all about SEEDS!

Heark Meadowlark
by Duane L. Herrmann

After woodpecker, blue
jay and cardinal, the first
bird I could know:
the meadowlark with
its bib and call,
now is named
in a farm renewing
seeds for preserving
genetic edible pool.

Photo: Meadowlark Hearth Farm by Agrarian Trust

Photo: Callie Walker Farm by Agrarian Trust

Callie Walker Farm

Farm, Sell, Give
by Leona Sevick

Wiping dusty hands on work shorts,
she settles into a straight backed
chair, smiles broadly. *My father knew
what all of his children would do
with their parcel of land.* I have not
met the others, but to me this
small woman, her blue eyes smiling
with interior light, has it
right. She will gift this rich land to
a family who will raise their
own clean food: red and black Angus,
Egyptian walking onions, meat
hens, radishes, carrots, comfrey.
She is the giver, or rather
the giver back. Pastor trained, she
will gift these green pastures, white-owned
but Black-worked, to the descendants
of the men and women whose tired
hands pulled all they could from this soil.
Can you see it? she asks, flushed and
alive. I swivel to look, think
yes I can. Yes, I really can.

Red Cow, Black Cow
by Leona Sevick

Once I thought I knew
what to make of cows,
their steady grazing
unchanged year by
year. I watch them chew
in clockwise motions,
their lips shiny with
work. They pay no mind
to my still form, my
scratching pencil as
they skim along an
emerald field, gently
tugging as they go.
My father raised cows
too, though he never
knew or thought to ask
what makes the red ones
so much bigger. She
tells me red coats are
cooler, permitting
them to graze longer
in the sun. I think
"luck of the draw." Their
lot, circumscribed by
color, by where the
ball decides to land.
I think, they aren't so
different from people,
though some of us have
choices to make. Let's
hope we choose wisely.

In Praise of Permaculture
by Leona Sevick

Praise the intelligent design
that suggests how we
live on this land
is also how we should
live with each other:

observe then interact
      catch and store what's precious
seek a good yield
      self-regulate and accept feedback
waste nothing
      design from good patterns
integrate don't segregate
      use small and slow solutions
value diversity
      value the marginal
respond constructively to change.

Praise the landholders who
seek to live in simple
ways that sustain the land—
ways that could save us all
from each other.

N.B. A section of this poem is based on David Holmgren's list of permaculture design principles.

Black Seed Agroecology Farm & Village
"Tscha-kole-chy" (c'ča'kól'či, "Whidbey Island")

Acknowledging the First Nations of c'ča'kól'či
("Tscha-kole-chy", Whidbey Island)

We respectfully acknowledge that we are meeting in **c'ča'kól'či** ("Tscha-kole-chy", Whidbey Island).

This is the ancestral homeland of the **sduhúbš** (Snohomish), Lower Skagit, Swinomish, and Suquamish First Nations of **x̌ʷʼəlč** ("hw`uhlch", Salt-Water, Puget Sound).

Each of these First Nations had well-established winter villages and seasonal harvesting territories on **c'ča'kól'či** at the time of the 1855 Point Elliott Treaty. For four long years, the United States Senate delayed ratifying the Point Elliott Treaty.

Meanwhile European and American settler-colonists rushed in, forcibly displacing the First Nations, and burning down their longhouses, in the absence of effective law enforcement. The First Nations on **c'ča'kól'či** were never compensated for their catastrophic losses.

We raise our hands to honor the **sduhúbš** (Snohomish), Lower Skagit, Swinomish, and Suquamish First Nations of on **c'ča'kól'či**. We thank them for their hospitality as the First People of this land, and for our continuing use of the natural resources of their Ancestral Homeland.

—Land Acknowledgement for Whidbey Island
Created in consultation with
The Snohomish Tribal Committee
of South Whidbey
July 2022
© 2022 Tom Speer

Poet's Introduction

These three poems were created by Catalina Marie Cantú, an Indigenous Mexican/Madeiran poet, as a homage to "Tscha-kole-chy" (**c'ča'kól'či,** "Whidbey Island"), whose First Nations considered her to be a Living Being.

These poems were not intended to speak in the place of Whidbey Island's First Nations, which in 1855 included the Snohomish, Lower Skagit, Swinomish, and Suquamish.

We raise our hands to honor "Tscha-kole-chy" (**c'ča'kól'či**, "Whidbey Island") and her First Nations.

—Catalina Marie Cantú
(with Duwamish Thomas Speer)
July 2, 2022

Photo by Aliko West

Poems by Catalina Marie Cantú

THE LAND: WHO I WAS

I was homeland to the **sduhúbš** (Snohomish) the First People who shared my island meadows. Field birds built nests among my bracken ferns, jade nettles, blue camas, and black mountain huckleberry.

I was Home, in every part with a purpose. Bracken roots ground into flour for bread. Nettles for medicine and dye with its bark rolled into two-ply string for fishing and duck nets. Camas' bulbs harvested like potatoes. Huckleberries dried.

I was Homelands, where my Douglas firs, Western Cedars, and Hemlocks touched the sky on a hill above my lower meadow. A forest for long houses, canoe building, and storm shelter. Past the forest, a clearing with a creek for family living, and ceremonies. Then, another forest where deer, elk, and bear were hunted for food, their skins good for Northwest winters.

I was Homelands, where the **x̌ʷ'əlč** was a short walk to saltwater clams, crabs, ducks, birds, and salmon. A bounty shared by First People in harmony with my nature. We respected and nurtured each other. After every fall harvest, fire cleared my lower meadow. The winter rain extinguished the flames.

I was Homelands.
For tens of thousands of years.
We believed it would last forever.

THE LAND: WHO I AM

Stolen
> from the children who played in my meadows and climbed my trees.
> No one asked me why
> they should not be sent to boarding schools.

Sold
> to a European family to raise cattle.
> I had never heard the word yet watched
> those creatures trample my meadows of bracken, camas, and nettles.

Fenced
> my forest that touched the sky
> and felled with axes and saws, dammed
> with dikes, another word I didn't know.

Zoned
> and divided by a highway, divided again
> into parcels. My new name Parcel 2, 089-235.
> 10.22 acres, a shadow of my former self.

Gifted
> as farmland, planted with fruit trees. Ignored.
> When was I ever a farm? That's the work
> of my neighbor, South Whidbey Tilth.

Leased
> for 99 years, a short time in my history,
> of the meadow's vernal pools
> nourishing my native plants.

THE LAND: WHO WILL I BE?

I am still homelands
to the **sduhúbš** (Snohomish).
Our spiritual connection
unbreakable.

While the creek sings
along my crown
without baby otters,

invasive mountain blackberries
strangle my meadows.
No bracken, camas, or nettles.

I watch
as deer and rabbit
follow their ancestral trails.

On my shoulder,
a fifty-foot hemlock
watches and waits.

She gives me courage
to believe
we have a future.

☼

Alternative Paths Forward
by Noah Wurtz

In an age defined by abstraction, where currencies like bitcoin make fortunes and politics unfold in the frenzied glow of the digital forum, land, our oldest and most reliable companion, remains at the center of everything.

Despite this, land is itself viewed in increasingly abstract terms. While billionaire investors see land as a stable asset to secure their wealth against volatile marketplaces, agribusinesses see it as a factory, calculating inputs to maximize outputs with little concern for the land's long term health, or its connection to the broader community. Even average Americans ascribe to an ideology of private land ownership, prioritizing innate individual rights to land over its real ecological, cultural, and economic connection to the broader landscape. Such an individualized, profit-oriented model of land use has led to the rapid loss of agricultural land, and the widespread destruction of our shared environment.

If we are to create a more resilient and equitable system of land tenure, we need new ways of thinking about the land, along with agile strategies that allow us to put these forms of thought into practice.

There has already been some incredible work done by regenerative and agroecological farmers, who connect their work explicitly with the overall wellbeing of the planet, and the creation of a just and equitable food system. Yet a full realization of this relational approach to land stewardship is impeded by a simple, but devastating fact. As land becomes increasingly expensive and concentrated in the hands of a few owners, farmers and their communities are presented with fewer and fewer opportunities to manage their land holistically. Instead, private ownership reduces land to a commodity that can be bought and sold at will, erasing the more complex interwoven values of land as a community and ecological asset and replacing them with a single monolithic imperative—profit at all costs.

It is more profitable, for example, to develop farmland into a new shopping center or residential development than it is to farm it. Today, nature appears to be losing to parking lots. As a result of real estate development, agricultural land is disappearing at a rate of 2000 acres per day.

Private ownership has led to the widespread misuse of land for the benefit of a small pool of real estate developers and agribusinesses, while disproportionately favoring a white, land owning class. Without widespread and equitable access to land, the work of farmers and communities seeking to create a more just and sustainable way of living on the land will continue to be severely limited.

Healthy land is essential to the survival of all life on Earth, and too valuable to be lost to development. A more wholistic ecological and ethical understanding of land begins with a more inclusive decision-making process. There is no need for us to start from scratch. Existing models, such as community land trusts and the Agrarian Commons are gaining momentum and serve as alternative paths forward, both for our species, and for those with whom we share the great natural web.

COMMUNITY ECOLOGY INSTITUTE

Community Ecology Institute
@ Freetown Farm

Maryland

VISION

Communities are healthy, resilient, abundant and rooted in regenerative relationships that honor the inherent interdependence between people and the ecosystems of which we are a part.

MISSION

Human and Natural Communities Thriving Together.

-Poets: Patti Ross and Laura Shovan
-Essayist: Chiara d'Amore

CEI's Journey to Land Stewardship

Founded in 2016, the Community Ecology Institute (CEI) is a Maryland-based non-profit with a mission to cultivate communities where people and nature thrive together. Our vision is that all communities are healthy, resilient, abundant and rooted in regenerative relationships that honor the inherent interdependence between people and the ecosystems of which we are a part. Through our mission, programs, advocacy, and engagement, CEI joyfully advances ecosystem health for the lasting protection of living beings. Our diverse, inclusive community nourishes both social connection and our inherent connection with the earth. Collaboratively, we foster the replenishing skills and relationships needed for people to live more lightly, responsive to climate change and fueled by our interdependence.

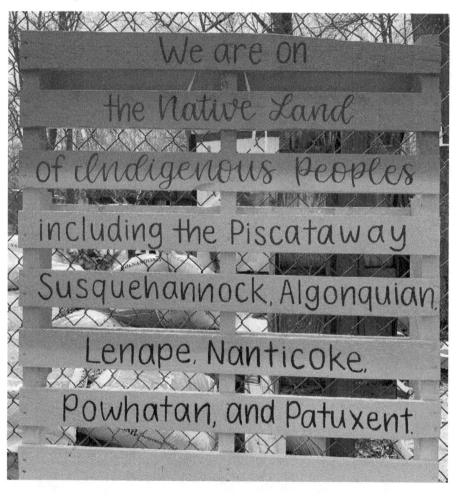

In all of our work, CEI's guiding principles are as follows:

1.   Inclusive Belonging. Everyone wants to be part of something bigger than themselves. Creating a space where all people feel worthy, honored, and respected based upon our shared humanity is a fundamental component of healthy community-building. In such spaces, people can work with vigor and trust to address deeply rooted problems, healing social and ecological wounds that can only be solved through collective empowerment.

2.   Restorative Reciprocity. CEI's policies, communication, and practices follow a restorative system design in which relationships are built and maintained with respect, gratitude, and learning. These relationships include those we share with the natural world. CEI models stewardship through engaging in sustainable practices. Teaching about these practices is an integral part of our programs, services, and operations.

3.   Health and Wellness. CEI approaches all organizational decisions as opportunities to support individual and collective health and wellness. This includes the design of programs, the care of our team, and the stewardship of our land. Advancing health and wellness is core to our organization's mission.

4.   Integrity & Accountability. CEI is invested in creating positive change and as such is committed to transparency, honesty and self-improvement. The organization acknowledges faults as part of an intentional learning process. The resilient trust necessary for any thriving community is a trust that must be earned.

In addition to being rooted in these principles, CEI's work is rooted in the research associated with its founder's doctoral research in sustainability education, which focused on creating the conditions for social and environmental connection and care. This work built on a substantial body or research identifying three foundational life experiences shared by adults who demonstrate an active commitment to environmental care:

1.   time spent enjoying nature as a child

2.   a person who role-modeled appreciation for nature

3.   participation in a nature- or environment-focused organization that offered direct learning opportunities

CEI was founded to make real-world use of these findings—to develop and celebrate environmental stewards—people who actively cherish nature's profound reciprocities. To this end, we focus on tangible, community-level change at the intersections of environment, education, equity, and health and concentrate on four Cs: Connection to Nature, Civic Ecology, Community Health, and Climate Action. We teach and showcase evidence-based best practices that are specifically responsive to our community's natural and social ecosystems. We also develop resources for other communities (e.g., counties, towns) and community-based organizations (e.g., school systems, civic groups) to help them effectively engage those they serve in nature-based opportunities that enhance individual and community well-being.

In the first two years of CEI's existence, we were running two nature-based experiential education programs that continue today. Columbia Families in Nature provides weekly opportunities for local families to explore and interact with nature together. Through CFIN, we aim to foster a life-long love and appreciation for the environment in the lives of local families while promoting deeper connection in their family unit, and with the community. Our Roots & Wings Learning Community (R&W) program provides homeschooled children with experiential, nature-based supplemental education programs that nurture their knowledge, creativity and unique voices.

As a result of the positive impact of these founding programs in their first few years, in the summer of 2018 CEI was given the opportunity to purchase a 6.4-acre farm in the city of Columbia to protect it from housing development and make it accessible to the community. The President of CEI's Board of Director's tells the story of this huge leap of faith in her own words here:

The land CEI now stewards seemed to find us. In 2018, CEI was only two years old and operating on a shoestring budget, yet our mission and initial nature-based programs had smitten local imaginations. On the summer solstice, an intriguing email arrive at CEI: a local farmer, David Shaw, didn't want his small suburban farm developed and was looking for someone who would buy it, but keep it in agricultural use. Owner of the last working farm in Columbia, Maryland, Shaw had lovingly and organically sustained a community supported agriculture program for 40 years on 6.4 fertile acres in the Middle Patuxent watershed—land in the heart of what had once been a community called Freetown. Over those decades, Shaw Farms welcomed more than 80 local families to 8000 Harriet Tubman Lane throughout each growing season to collect squash and tomatoes, herbs and kale. Its soil grew rich with compost. Shaw had even begun to build a home for his aging parents on the property, but they passed before he could finish and the project was paused indefinitely. Over time, blackberry and rose brambled the woods as mugwort and dock took over the crop rows. A townhouse development was constructed on adjacent property. Knowing he could not farm indefinitely yet longing to keep his land protected, Shaw quietly spoke to some colleagues in the community, people who promised to be on the lookout for just the right buyer. He did not list the property publicly. He cast a few seeds of hope. One of which landed with CEI's founder, Dr. Chiara D'Amore, in that email entitled "I hear you are looking for a farm." Over the course of exactly one year, CEI's small team (no staff!) and robust community, took a big leap of faith and

rallied together to raise the funds needed to purchase the farm. Working with a team of connected community members from the Leadership Howard County program, CEI was able to bring together the Howard County government, city of Columbia, the Conservation Fund, and hundreds of individual donors to meet our fundraising goal. During the week of the summer solstice of 2019, Dr. D'Amore and Mr. Shaw signed the development restricted deed to transfer the farm to CEI's stewardship. The last three years have been an incredible journey of growth as we get to know the land and create a space where people can learn from direct experience about how to lead happier, healthier, more connected and sustainable lives.

One of our initial ways of engaging the community in our care of this land was to ask for input from the people who helped us purchase and protect it on what it should be named. We got hundreds of recommendations, but ultimately settled on Freetown Farm to honor the history of the land and our hopes for how it can inform the future.

Freetown Farm's History

Today, what is known as Freetown Farm is a 6.4 acre organic farm located in a historic African-American community within the city of Columbia Maryland. The farm is less than a quarter of a mile from the Middle Patuxent River and includes a variety of ecosystems, including fields, meadows, woods, wetlands, and two small streams. If you do an internet search on the area, one of the first things that pops up is a Wikipedia post that says "People and nature have long flourished beside the Middle Patuxent River. Over 12,000 years ago, Native Americans hunted deer and gathered acorns and other wild food in the woods and waters. People from Woodland Indian cultures settled nearby approximately 2,000 years ago, leaving traces of their lives in the earthenware pottery and stone tools they left behind." Written land records for this area trace back to the 1630s, when European colonizers began laying claim to the traditional land of local Native American tribes, including the Piscataway Conoy, Susquehannock, Algonquian, Lenape, Nanticoke, Powhatan, and Patuxent People. Conflict increased as colonists continued to encroach on tribal lands, culminating in the first treaty in 1666 to establish the Piscataway reservation. This was followed by subsequent treaties, all of which would be broken in the coming years, resulting in the cruel loss of native homelands.

By 1690, records show that the plantations of this area used the labor of enslaved people, often for the growing and harvesting of tobacco. Once iron ore was discovered, slave labor was used in mining to support railroads. When asked what role enslaved people played in developing Howard County, Wylene Burch, the founding director of the Howard County Center of African American Culture explained: "They built it. All of these buildings built in the 1700s, they must have used the slave trade to build them. Those people really struggled and worked and developed this area." Slavery had been inflicted in Howard County for more than 150 years when, in 1845, local landowner Nicolas Worthington died and, in his will, manumitted seventeen people he had enslaved and gave them the ability to live freely on 150 acres of land—an area that became known as Freetown. It is important to note however, that formal ownership of this land was willed to the prominent white Clark family.

According to the 1860 Census, more than one in five Howard County residents was an enslaved person. Another 10 percent were free black people—double the proportion of the rest of the state. Local historians believe that Freetown and the surrounding community of Simpsonville served as an important stopover point in the Underground Railroad. Ms. Burch noted research that showed the Underground Railroad thrived in Howard County because it was in "the tight place" as slaves moved north through Maryland via different waterways, such as the Middle Patuxent and Patapsco rivers.

CEI's farm on Harriet Tubman Lane sits at the intersection of three locations on the Freetown-Simpsonville Legacy Trail known to have been part of the Underground Railroad. Slavery in Maryland was not abolished until the state legislature took action on November 1, 1864, almost two years after the Emancipation Proclamation.

Throughout the 1800s and into the mid-1900s, this area was largely agricultural, which informed the livelihoods and opportunities of the people living in Freetown and the surrounding Simpsonville area. Our specific tract of land was owned by the Clark family until 1898, when it was purchased by Essex Mokin, then a number of people in the Boardly family until 1921 when it transferred to the Dorsey family until purchased by the Shaw family in 1981. Mr. Shaw noted that he was the first white person to live in the community for quite some time. From 1963 to 1966, The Rouse Company purchased large tracts of farmland in the area to develop what was to become the city of Columbia. The vision of Columbia, a unique planned community, was to create a city that was "a garden for the growing of people." From its inception, Columbia championed integration—across race, class, and faith. The city's iconic "People Tree" statue embodies this vision of our inter-connectedness. At Freetown Farm, the last working farm with a Columbia address, we aim to honor the rich legacies in our soil.

Stewarding Freetown Farm

In the three years that CEI has been the stewards of Freetown Farm, most of it under the duress of the Covid-19 pandemic, CEI has transformed the property from its dormant state into a unique place of diverse common ground for our community. As the steward of this fertile land, CEI has been able to steadily expand the types of programs we offer and the populations we serve. The unprecedented food security and social isolation challenges that COVID dealt our community led us to focus on programs that nourish people's physical and mental health while always prioritizing the health of the land. As farmers, we are practicing regenerative agriculture, which is a restorative approach to food and farming systems that focuses on soil regeneration, increasing biodiversity, supporting watershed health, and increasing resilience to climate change. We are inspired by permaculture design and practice no-till gardening, have planted over 500 trees and shrubs, mostly native and edible, and created pollinator meadows.

FREETOWN FARM

Kiosk

Parking

Pollinator Garden

Bioretention Pond & Meadow

Rain Garden

Fire Pit

Chicken Coop

Beehives

Medicinal Herb Spiral

Wetlands

Makerspace

Restroom

Volunteer Tool Shed

Forest Restoration

Children's Play Area

Forest Stage

Mushroom Garden

Food Forest

Children's Garden

Office Space

Greenhouse 2

Community Engagement Center

Hopeworks Healing Garden

Market Garden

Grow It, Eat It Garden

NAACP Garden

Greenhouse 1

Farmstand/Welcome Area

Climate Victory Garden

Community Ecology Institute
@ Freetown Farm

Map by Hawke Reyes
All photos by Chiara D'Amore

One of our most successful projects has been around community stormwater management. Stormwater from neighboring Atholton High School is directed onto the farm via a culvert and underground pipe. The previous farm owner had simply piped this incoming water to the edge of the property, allowing the flooding and erosion in the neighborhood to continue southwest towards the Middle Patuxent River. Stormwater runoff from the school also flows across Harriet Tubman Lane and a bus yard and onto the farm, causing flooding for the farm as well as surrounding properties. From 2019 to 2021, CEI completed a three-part Chesapeake Bay Trust grant to address the stormwater from Atholton High School that flows on to Freetown Farm through the design and installation of a series of best management practices that feature a large bioretention pond designed to hold as much stormwater as possible. In 2020 we successfully started the Trust's Green Streets, Green Jobs, Green Towns (G3) grant series to develop a green stormwater infrastructure plan for Atholton High School. We have just received approval for the grant to implementation this design on the high school's property.

Together, these on and off-farm projects will provide highly visible demonstrations of BMPs, achieve health benefits for the Middle Patuxent Watershed, address chronic neighborhood stormwater flooding, and provide outdoor education spaces for the school and community. These projects are also essential to the larger Walkable Watershed Initiative that CEI co-created with the community to address stormwater management issues along with community needs and neighborhood quality of life goals, such as improved neighborhood connectivity, better access to vibrant outdoor spaces, and a sense of synergy among the community's diverse assets.

We work with numerous community partners to design and steward the farm to be a demonstration grounds for as many ecological best practices as possible. It is our goal that everyone who visits can come away inspired by direct action they can bring to their own homes and neighborhoods. A swale feeds into the bioretention pond, which is surrounded by a new native meadow, a rain garden collects water off of our northern greenhouse, and just outside the greenhouse is a kitchen herb garden. We have the second climate victory garden registered in the state of Maryland, which will soon be home to ground mounted

solar, to support our goal of being zero net energy by 2025. We host a
University of Maryland Grow It, Eat It Garden, stewarded by Master
Gardeners. The Howard County Branch of the National Association
for the Advancement of Colored People (NAACP) has a large garden
from which they have a community supported agriculture program. We
are a part of the global Transition Town movement and have a Maker
Space designed to help people reduce, reuse, recycle, repair, reskill and
reimagine their relationship with the products of daily life. We have
a large market garden, from which we have grown and shared over
10,000 pounds of food in the last two years. The local domestic violence
recovery center has a healing garden and a non-profit that supports
women of color entrepreneurs stewards and utilizes our medicinal herb
garden. Two bee keepers use Freetown Farm as an "out yard" and we
have a flock of chickens and two turtles that can't be released to the wild.
Our Roots & Wings program uses a larger youth garden and food forest
as their primary classroom space.

These investments and transformations have been the work of literally
thousands of people. Since purchasing the farm we have tracked the
participation of over 1750 different people who have volunteered on
the property! Especially given the challenges of Covid, our volunteer
program has offered people a unique outdoor setting where they feel
safe, connected, supported in their well-being, and part of collective care.
We emphasize being accessible and welcoming to the full diversity of
our community – people of all ages and backgrounds and abilities – and
are proud of and grateful for the unique place of common ground that
Freetown Farm has become for our full community. Here is a testimonial
from the parent of a differently-abled regular volunteer at Freetown
Farm in 2021: "Volunteering at Freetown Farms is the highlight of K--'s
week! Though he cannot tell us with words all that he enjoys, we can feel
it in his excited rush to get out of the car each Wednesday, and hear it in
his laughter as he waters the plants, pulls weeds, or plants seeds. If you
ask him what he does at the farm, he simply answers, 'help the plants.'
That's purpose! It's a win-win really. K-- has helped and, at the same time,
Freetown Farms has given him a meaningful opportunity to work. Thank
you to everyone who has welcomed him and made Freetown Farms such
a positive place to be!"

Roots, Wings, and Rise

All of CEI's programs are now rooted at Freetown Farm, including our original Families in Nature and Roots & Wings programs. By the end of 2021, the CFIN program had offered 278 free events that were enjoyed by 9,300 participants and equated to more than 20,000 hours outside. The Roots & Wings program started as a two day a week program in a local rec room and served twenty families. In 2021, the program welcomed 86 children to the program and added an "upper" program for kids aged 10 to 13 who are growing up with Roots & Wings.

In the fall of 2020, CEI launched what is now known as our Root & Rise Student Internship Program at Freetown Farm, which has two tracks: one for high-school students in Howard County and one for college students in the region. The high-school track draws students via two paths. First, 15-20 applicants are invited to participate in our year-long program, which provides robust experiential environmental education and community engagement opportunities. The students in this facet of our program work together both after school and on weekends to help steward Freetown Farm. They are guided in learning about and taking leadership on initiatives such as: native tree planting and food forestry; creating native pollinator meadows; stormwater management best practices and their maintenance; stream monitoring; garden design, creation, maintenance and harvesting; reducing and reusing waste materials; plant propagation; animal and plant species identification; and community engagement and communications around ecological stewardship. Each week, these core interns provide more than 50 hours of combined service, engaging in their own environmental exploration and education, applying that knowledge to projects, and sharing their knowledge with other community members and volunteers.

The high-school internship program also serves neuro-diverse students participating in a range of programs provided by the public school system. These interns ride by bus to the farm two-to-four days per week during their school day and are supported by CEI and school system staff to learn transferable job skills. Our college internship program is coordinated directly with programs and professors aligned with our mission. As one participant described it: "My internship experience at the Community Ecology Institute has been full of engaging and exciting experiences. I got to join a team of diverse individuals and connect myself with the vibrant, local community. From networking and research to carpentry and cultivation, CEI's breadth of possibilities facilitates their mission for both personal and community growth. During my internship, I've witnessed the incredible moments of teamwork and unity, laughter and joy, and harmony amongst everyone here — from the new volunteers to the veteran staff. CEI is a unique combination of flexibility, support, and positivity, creating an irresistible feeling of positivity within the organization." To date, more than four dozen youth have participated in CEI's internship program, most of whom have been students of color.

Nourishing Gardens

In 2021 CEI launched our Nourishing Gardens program, which has two primary goals: transforming lawns into ecologically beneficial, food-growing gardens; and providing experiential learning and workforce development opportunities. CEI selected 15 trainees ranging in age from 16 to 60 to participate in our inaugural 10-week intensive experiential learning curriculum designed to prepare people—no matter their previous experience with gardening—with the knowledge and skills necessary to plan, prepare, and install Nourishing Gardens throughout the community. At the start of the training, the Nourishing Gardens team worked at Freetown Farm to add trees and shrubs to a food forest, plant fall crops in the market garden, and plant native, pollinator-supporting plants around our new bio-retention pond. After gaining experience and confidence with these on-farm installations, trainees applied their experience to community-based projects, including planting and care of gardens at elementary and middle schools and in city parks, as well as establishing a publicly accessible food garden at the community college. Trainees who have completed the program may be considered for an installation team lead position in future Nourishing Gardens training sessions; the program thus expands local green infrastructure workforce opportunities. This initiative won the Howard County Changemaker Challenge Community Choice Award by a wide margin. As one program participant summarized, "The Nourishing Garden program is incredibly thorough and filled with deep, rich teaching shared in a kind, passionate, and supportive community. I am so excited for the program to grow and for other families across our community to experience the immense joy and healthy satisfaction of growing their own food in their own yards!" In 2022, the Nourishing Gardens program is training 20 garden installers of diverse backgrounds and focusing on getting gardens in the ground at Title 1 schools throughout our community.

Across our initiatives and programs, CEI's recognizes that lands stewardship is justice work and our approach emphasizes individual and community empowerment and resiliency by providing nature-based experiential education. When it comes to addressing the intersectional issues of environmental justice, being rooted at a farm offers CEI a meaningful and universal entry point to engagement – food. We believe that food justice is when communities are able to exercise their right to grow, sell, and eat healthy food that is fresh, nutritious, affordable, culturally-appropriate, and grown locally with care for the well-being of the land, workers, and animals. Through our work at Freetown Farm and in our community programs, we are both teaching people how to grow their own food and increasing access to fresh produce grown where people live, learn, work and play. This work supports the physical and mental health of our community members, protects and restores the environment on which we depend, and takes steps towards food sovereignty, in which a priority is placed on generating healthy food for people, building knowledge and skills, working with nature, valuing food providers and localizing food systems, and honoring the cultural importance of food in our lives. We believe that communities able to achieve these goals are on their way to being modern "free towns".

On Seeing a Proliferation of Mayapples at Freetown Farm
by Laura Shovan

U'niskwetu''gǐ:
In Cherokee, its name means "it wears a hat."
We acknowledge that we are on the traditional land
of the Piscataway Conoy Tribe
as well as the Susquehannock, Algonquian, Lenape,
Nanticoke, Powhatan, and Patuxent peoples.

Indian apple:
A single white flower hangs
under shield-shaped leaves.
Maryland's first colonial governor
claimed this land. No treaty
can shield the loss of home
when treaties can be broken.

Devil's apple:
On this site, plantations
used the labor of enslaved people
to grow and harvest tobacco.
Foragers found the mayapple,
its golden fruit hiding
under poison leaves.

American mandrake:
In 1845, a landowner freed
seventeen people he had enslaved,
gave them this mandate—
150 acres of land belonged to them.
They called it Freetown.

Umbrella plant:
Spring ephemeral, shading these woods
in green. Its names shape the story
of Freetown Farm.

Blueberries: Interview and Found Poem
by Laura Shovan

*"Blueberries, native to North America, have been part of life here for 13,000 years.
Native Americans were the first to recognize the versatility and health benefits of
blueberries, using them for medicinal purposes and as natural flavoring."*
                    —*U.S. Highbush Blueberry Council, online May 2022*

I love blueberry bushes. It's linked very much to my childhood. **Growing
up** my father was from New England. Every summer we would go and
visit my grandmother in rural Connecticut. And the one thing we'd
do every summer is go blueberry **picking** with her. She had blueberry
bushes in her yard but we always went somewhere for blueberry picking,
which made it feel special. I remember her saying, "One for me and one
for the basket."

And then we'd come home and it would be a whole day of canning and
pie making and eating them fresh and finding different ways to use them.
The first thing that my grandmother really taught us about was picking
blueberries and making these wonderful things. That time as a small
child next to her learning there wasn't anything that went to waste. **Every
last blueberry** was going to be **used** that day. I love to make homemade,
fancy Pop-tarts, blueberry rhubarb with lemon glaze.

Kids just express whatever is on their mind almost instantly when they
taste something new. There's something so wonderful about the simple
reaction. Blueberries are a nice one because they're something that I don't
know that every kid loves. They're a little bit sour and have a little bit of
a bitter skin, but then also there is this total joy when you see them find
one at the farm.

To a certain extent almost all of my work now just reminds me how
important it was for me as **a child** to be **in nature** with people I loved,
teaching me lessons through hands-on work. So many valuable lessons
come out of **gardening**. The empathy you build by **looking at plants**
and trying to figure out what they need to grow and flourish. They're in
this environment that isn't always of their **choosing** and you want to give
them the best care you can while they live. My mother made it clear that

this plant you put here—it's your responsibility to take care of it. There's this great tie between the reciprocation you have with caring for plants and their gift to you **as a food source**.

In the fall their leaves just change colors ever so slightly. They go from green to an orange red and it just makes them so **beautiful**. They have these gorgeous little, tiny white flowers that the bees love, which is **joyful**. Picking **blueberries** is like the first, **real** coming-of-**summer** moment.

—*Theresa Taylor, Community Ecology Institute Nourishing Gardens Program Director, May 2022*

Growing up
picking blueberries—
every last berry used.
A child in nature
gardening
looking at plants
choosing this plant
as a food source.
Beautiful, joyful blueberries:
real summer.

Skunk Cabbage: Interview and Found Poem
by Laura Shovan

"The skunk cabbage is a flowering perennial plant and is one of the first plants to emerge in the spring. The flowers appear before the leaves and are characterized by a mottled maroon hoodlike leaf called a spathe.... As the flowers mature, the spathe opens more to allow pollinators such as flies and carrion beetles to enter and pollinate the flowers."

—National Wildlife Federation, online May 2022

There's a space at the farm filled with skunk cabbages.

I don't think I had an awareness of skunk cabbage until **I started** leading Columbia Families in Nature. As the leader of those events, I was always looking for things that I could point out to people. There's a real effort I make **to notice** the small things that other people might walk by.

In the time of year that skunk cabbage comes out, there is so little to see that is **new life**. That's really a January, February time when they emerge. They're mottled purple and yellow-spotted when the rest of forest floor is brown and there's not much to see. Visually they're interesting. They're something to look for **in that bleak time of year**. They almost look like swamp lilies, kind of like calla lilies.

The more I took notice in learning about **skunk cabbage**, the more my affinity for them grew. What's really cool about skunk cabbages is that they're **like tiny greenhouses**. The shape almost looks like a cupped hand or a harder-skinned lily. In its center there is like **a biochemical** reaction that creates heat and a smell that is very attractive to early spring, late winter pollinators. They're attracted to the pollen and the heat. Later in spring, they're in full leafy bloom, but it's the part that's like a swamp lily that I get excited about. My joy is when I'm hunting around very low, looking for those emergent swamp lilies. You have to be looking closely. It's this really cool treat to have as the benefit for paying close attention. It's cool to watch these plants over time. They have this **metamorphosis**. They don't look anything alike from start to finish. These massive leaves bigger than the size of your head. Kids get excited when skunk cabbages are big, leafy, and abundant. I'll break off a leaf and crush it, so they get

that skunky scent. Kids will say "Ew! Ew!" but it's with joy.

They are good from an erosion control perspective. They put down deeper roots year after year. They help anchor that part of the ecosystem. As they leaf out, they create shading and protection for other species— the tadpoles in the ephemeral ponds—helps keep those areas from drying out quickly in the full sun.

You have to look. As I get to know these plants, especially the ephemerals, going to visit them when they're in bloom is one of the best ways I know to ground and tether myself in a world where there's so much going on. It **anchors me in** the cyclical **nature** of things. It feels hopeful that they keep coming back.

—*Chiara D'Amore, Community Ecology Institute Executive Director, May 2022*

I started to notice
new life in that bleak
time of year.

Skunk cabbage
like tiny greenhouses—
a biochemical
metamorphosis.

That skunky scent
anchors me
in nature.

Freetown Farm Gardens (Sestina)
by Patti Ross

There are gardens here weaved in between a road of pebbles.
We were walking Angela and I heading toward the forest
finding a wood stage surrounded by log seats children at play.
The lush green of the trees drawing us closer we almost missed her
an Isabella Tiger Moth or Banded Woolly bear no bigger than our thumb
creeping along mulch chips heading toward the Mushroom garden.

There are six gardens for eating and few others for healing all are
gardens.
There is much to see and do here at this free farm, a rain garden of
pebbles,
wildflowers fill the space with yellow and pink petals the size of my
thumb.
Chiara told us a Black bear was once among the Black Cherry trees of
the forest
I would have been scared if I saw a bear nearby but not her
my friend Angela is fearless, nothing bothers her or end her play.

The homeschool kids have arrived and what is learning looks like play.
I remember I used to make mud pies pretending to sell them at Market
Garden.
We both went to school in Philadelphia, but I am not as courageous as
her.
Near the Medicinal Herb Spiral, I saw the Ricinus plant still walking the
pebbles
leaves with what seemed streaked blood overshadowed the circumstantial
forest
moving toward the plant I held the big leaf between my finger and right
thumb.

Wetlands behind the herb spiral have cattails thick and thin as my thumb
they are singing in this purposeful pond propagating as play
I never thought I would see so much on this little 6.4-acre farm and
forest.
Wetlands and their creeping roots sit next to the NAACP garden

where roots conjure up slaves moving quietly among the berm's pebbles.
I think back to the Woolly bear and wondering how many of her

Have survived the running feet of children overlooking her
while dancing to the Children's Garden to measure peppers thumb
sized and watch farm chickens peck among the pebbles
for crumbs left from lunchbox sandwiches lost at play
Screams and whispers tune my ears to the Grow it, Eat it Garden
remembering when I first became an explorer in the red clay Carolina
forest.

All this history, all this learning, carved out of this small forest
Looking at the big old Oak I ask: Did you see her?
Harriett! You know, all those times she passed this land of gardens.
Did she stop to rest here and lean against you leaving her thumb print?
Did those following her ask to rest in the lush giving worry away to play
to drink from the river Patuxent calming heart beats among the pebbles.

At noon, the is sun reflects off the forest river and paints glitter on its
pebbles
that sparkle, like squeals of homeschool kids out of the garden and off
to play.
Isabella, what a pretty name for a caterpillar no bigger than my thumb.

Castor-Oil's Apparition
by Patti Ross

Walking this farm path, I hear a whisper or was it more a soft call.
Strong to my hearing, a graceful ghost song?

Shifting toward garden plot where plants and herbs dwell between the
Forget-Me-Nots. Daydreaming of grandfather, walking his farm, my
hand in his hand callous and soft.

I saw her the *Ricinus communis* standing tall at the back of the garden box.
We had met before but not on this farm's pathway.

A different pathway down south where old folk in tribal talked of your
sacred purpose. Now understanding my aquiver on this Freetown Farm
parcel.

Empath, to tell the tale of African Queens and African Kings who
worked this land, using the crown of hair burying a seed for birthing in a
new land on bended knees.

The castor bean calming bodies pain used in the labor of bringing about
new life, new generations. Hands praying of luminous parables filling
new days of hope then evoking its origin - East Africa.

Sitting on beach in Tanzania, or the market in Uganda combing windblown hair.

Writing the Land Mondo
by Patti Ross and Laura Shovan

Patti's Questions & Laura's Responses

How can the roots of
a cherry tomato plant
hold the weight of poverty?

> Nourished soil is rich
> with nutrients, water, sun—
> nourished humans thrive like vines.

On knees, weeding, what
societal albatross have
we fought to unearth today?

> Backs exposed to sun—
> memory of growing food
> in pogroms and plantations.

The Red-winged blackbird
watches Harriett; did she just
whisper the route to freedom?

> Follow her red flash:
> a sash tied to a low branch,
> a quilted curve of crimson.

Will we find fertile
seeds of social justice in
the terse catechism of plants?

> Rows of collards, kale—
> a psalm composed of new life
> feeds our souls, fills our bellies.

Laura's Questions & Patti's Responses

When you put your hands
in farm soil, what legacy
gets trapped underneath your nails?

> The tears of Tribal
> leaders and the bloody sweat
> of African Kings.

If this land could speak
its history, what stories
would its dark, tangled roots spell?

> Worthington, Clark, Shaw,
> 17 humans enslaved until free.
> Tubman unafraid.

Who walked here, who worked,
hid, and died on Freetown's fields?
Whose lives make this land fertile?

> Brits, Indigenous,
> enslaved and free. All ate of
> the native persimmon trees.

F.A.R.M.S.

EARMS

South Carolina

Our mission is to provide rural family farmers with legal support while reducing hunger in the farmers community

-Rosa Parks Farmers Market—Doris Frazier; Jillian Hishaw
-The Males Place—Malyk Rowell; Doris Frazier; Jillian Hishaw
-F.A.R.M.S.—Jillian Hishaw

Photo: Negro sharecropper with twenty acres. Library of Congress, Prints & Photographs Division, FSA/OWI Collection, [LC-DIG-fsa-8b32339]; by Dorothea Lange, June 1938

F.A.R.M.S. — Muskogee, OK

On Bended Knees
by Jillian Hishaw

Like the death of the Lakota at Wounded Knee

we scream for the centuries

...the bleeding.

in death, their spirits we envy

in lands full of freedom, in earth and breeze

soil fertilized with the blood of our ancestors that whisper in the trees.

paper annexing stolen dirt

white immigrants' wealth.

white immigrants
black hands
stolen lands

mixed up mules and crows and miles and acres of land yet to sow
it's happening now - did you know?

for the "freed" enslaved for their mothers, fathers
today there is more bleeding

all the wrongs are still too white
losing 30,000 acres
losing rights.

the losing non-whites

from the five uncivilized
my people were mixed, sold, never found
the five tribes built up by pounding the backs of my family down

my freedoms?
my people.
the land will tell you a story

after the rain, after the tears, the soil is one way to turn black the years

of course, now, post pandemic, to dust it gets plowed, after the trail the loophole that infests the rest for money. Money. Land.

step back on black backs to get ahead in a supremacy system of tactical land theft that is ruled on in precedence's at the highest courts

my fight is my right against this supremacist...system. weighing in at 6 to 2. I am a servant still. Civil.

with the land in our hands, we hold on

on our bended knees we hold on

for 30,000 acres

disguised as a tax lien void of conservation and hope

strokes on reserved land not held in trust

no trust

for the predator

I'm coming.

with a soft voice and a black pen

with my ancestors behind me

for the land that was earned.

honor the deed once prayed for on bended knees

F.A.R.M.S.—Kern County, CA

Cheap Food Pickers
by Jillian Hishaw

Hooray! For slave wages in 2022 exploitation by the White man still exists

Step right up! Step right up!

Buy a worker for $50.00 or an immigrant willing to work for free, not caring about how much they get paid…supposedly.

They say the immigrant only cares about how much they can send home to support their family because conditions in their country are at times not even our worst.

But before you blame the immigrants, you need to look at the origin of the hurt.

It's the partison politics steady causing the trouble

Just because they contribute to the political campaign, the melanated majority has to suffer.

Still livin as a slave, in a two-room shack getting paid what their father did in 1946, equivalent to $2.66 without tax only difference is instead of picking cotton, they pick fruit for not enough to buy their own family food.

The commercials say "support a child for $25.00 a day" but what about the kids that are being exploited for a slave wage?

Why don't people think about who picks the food that goes into their mouth, as the rolls around their body steady expands out.

Migrant workers have to live from hand to mouth as ag expenditure go South.

The complexities of "cheap food" as 99 percent of the soil is now eroded, to line the pockets of the political, White elite who now plan to make billons off lab meat.

As the true minority never reveals the truth, that this is another control tactic to deny the pickers with two-tone complexion food.

F.A.R.M.S. – Wilcox County, AL

Alabama
by Jillian Hishaw

I'm still in Alabama

My heart will always be in the state

Even though, I physically have lived elsewhere for years,

I will never forget the tears that night, when we were forced to take flight

After a cross was lit, we split up and out. Three went East, Two went North, and None stayed South. Like a thief in the night our farm was gone.

However, our ancestors are still embedded in the red clay soils of Wilcox County, plot 44 off of Hwy 28 West

No rest since then after being forced off the land we held so dear, until a White woman got raped and all hell broke loose the Smith family being the only ones to lose.

The land that we held in deed and trust for 40 years straight, is now thought of in tears. But as I reminisce, I hold memories of Alabama in love.

The smell of butter beans and ox tail stew.....brings me back to simple times that we will never get back

My memories are beyond the attack, and I will always have fond memories of the great state that we long to move back.

The Males Place—Charlotte, NC

Untitled
by Malyk Rowell

Saturday morning, Up bright and early on the way to The Male's Place
                                                                    Garden,
8am SHARP, we're expected to make haste and never to be late
Beginning with a fresh breeze of the day
We hope to finish early so we may play
For we have learned, "Work Hard First, then you can relax and enjoy the
                                                                    day"
for this is called priority and responsibility, values instilled within us
during all our days

The Male's Place Garden, a place of nourishment of the body as well as
                                                                    the soul

Planting seedlings of responsibility, we groom ourselves with
                                                            accountability,
Of a man who own his mistakes with sincerity

Growing seedlings of maturity, we carry ourselves at all times with pride
                                                                and dignity
By walking in the footsteps of our elders, learning from their authenticity

Sprouting wildly at times and growing slowly at others
The work in the garden is never over
Yet our roots continue to grow, thicken, and spread
Digging deep into the earth – as we each mature into a man

Working together, UMOJA
Thru the toil of our sweat, we become stronger
Working together, UJIMA
Thru the tilling of the soil, we confront our challenges
Working together, IMANI
Thru the faith and determination of our harvest, we build strong black
men for the betterment of our community

The Male's Place Garden -
Though the blessings you have bestowed upon us may not yet be
realized directly in today's picture
we pray you hear your adulations now as we know your blessings will
abound in the future

Country Playground
by Doris Frazier

My Auntie Say...

The Land loves children
As its fans
With their joy/laughter
innocent exploring hands
Running feet/that beat
A Rhythm/familiar sweet
Children Understand

My Auntie Say...

Back in her childhood day
Made trips to her Grandparents farm

Memories!
Touching the Land
any way we can
Running through corn fields
with outstretched arms/hands
wearing bare feet
A special treat
Sifting Gray Sand

Awww !
We were writing the land

With gritty footprints
and sticky sweat hands

The Land's
Sister Sun was Blazing Hot
Stop Playing ? Not!

My Auntie Say ...

Echoing - Loud Yelling Cousins
was allowed
WOW!

No commands... 'Stop running' /'Be quiet'
It was Grand

My grandparents "owned" their
land
My Auntie Say...
with Pride

All day/love to play outside
In deep country playground
Big and wide

As far as I could see
the land belonged to me

Riding in bumpy wagons
We all 'squeezin' fit
Finding wood
Digging holes
For yard barbeque pit

Grandma called out
Time to eat

Our garden was our store

Right outside (on nature's floor)
Ground space/ the place
To harvest/plant own food
Fresh greens/beans
tomatoes sweet
Fresh picked berries
walnut from the trees
Honey from the bees

My Auntie Say ...

Country Summer.... Fun
For me
The Land... My Liberty
For down home cousins/hard work
not just play
The land/ their life
of every day
Planting/cropping/plowing
Sowing
And
Laughing/Loving/Connecting/Knowing
This is my Land

Auntie tell me more
about Before

Auntie Say..

At age 10
Planted my own little garden
To watch it grow

Teach me Auntie
I Want to Know

Garden Men
by Jillian Hishaw, Esq.

Boys will be boys, so they say
But for the young men of the Males Place this is not true

Young men being raised to know the truth about the history of the land
We cultivated from the African Diaspora that was consecrated

We learn to lift our voices as we learn how to plow the city fields
With love and admiration, we fill each basket to give to the community
the male leadership it needs
As we plant the seed each year to grow more perennials as we annually
acknowledge the most high.

Thanking the City for the soils and the Baba Reggie for his dedication as
we grow from boys to men in each season of growth.

Rosa Parks Farmers Market – Charlotte, NC

The Land Writes Itself
by Doris Frazier

Unconditionally/
Truthfully/
Nutritionally/
Lovingly/
Tearfully/
Joyously/
Defensively/
Freely/
Bountifully/
Wholly/
Peacefully/
Passionately/
Historically/
Creatively/
Nature (ally)/
The Land 'writes' itself/
The Human 'Rights' self/
We Journey to connect and reflect the 'Truth' in
All

☼

Land of Good and Plenty
by Doris Frazier

Oh, Land of Good and Plenty
How do you hold us all ...
So Many

Some get Good and Plenty

Yet
Others are sad 'without any'

Oh Land of Good and Plenty
You are the Keeper of Tales
and Stories
Our Triumphs/our Glories
Our Torrids/our Horrids

You provide space
for our birth place

You swallow us up
in death
To replenish yourself as one
So we keep on Be-ing
Born to do and get done

You take abuse
For our use
' Til the sunset has won / day done
Then day breaks
A new day awaits...

Grateful !
Still here
With depths and widths/
heights/varied soil textures/
colors that do matter

and shine your worth
You ... our floor of Earth

For the land of plenty
No more has grown
But we must go on

Blood washed away by tears
of Tyranny/war/selfishness/
greed/
We fight over you/for you/
take sides/ plead wants and
needs
Yet...
We all appear/same one mouth open
To partake/ For Life's Sake
Our sustenance
From the land of Good and Plenty

Some get Plenty
Others   "not any"

Our Southern Plains...
Now...

The Great Gold "Rush Land'/terrain
Where land is captured/claimed
not much remains
not growing more land
Seizures /poor sales
Bad deals are made
Un-informed owners /hands tied
Too late to (real eyes)

Where do victims go
When bad showers begin to
r-e-i-g-n

Blessed!
with those like Atty. Jillian
travels our country/other lands
to lend a skillful hand
to farmers/others who need a plan
She's there!
to advise/inform/represent
her passionate efforts well-spent

Who survives?
Those left standing
to "take" a stand
Again and Again

Energized by our young
with new creations/innovations for us ...
And
The land of Good and Plenty

A 'Lot' of Land
by Doris Frazier

Welcome to the Rosa Parks
Farmers Market ! (Charlotte, NC)

Writing the land with Historical Marks
Like famed civil rights Leader
Rosa Parks

The Marketorians
Fighting for continuous existence and improvement
with unique approaches to their movement

Rosa Parks Quote:
When ones mind is made up, this diminishes fear
(knowing what must be done)

The Rosa Parks Farmers Marketorians
Showing up/not giving up
Creating legacy /for community
Inventing Solutions/for Family needs
Resulting/Harmony
No Dis-ease

An Art Form/Can't Die
To sustain/strengthen
To feed our bodies/mind/spirit/soul
Never gets old

Welcome to
'A lot' of Land
 On the West end

Let's give
a shout or two
for the ones that show up and do
to name a few

Farmer (land owner) Paul Brewington
of a 4th generation
Standing Giant in Height
and Grace /at his place
Behind table of Home Grown
Veggies delight/Fruit
Watermelon always "Right"

Bernice Smith (age 83)
Queen mother market planner/supporter
Yippee!
Brings Wisdom/Love/Stories/Laughter
She gardens/cooks /like no other
Taught at age 8 by her blind farming grandmother

Shout/Shout
the young men (of school age)
organization/The Males Place
Who Brighten their market space
Grow their garden/beautiful greens
Baba Reggie/Sharman Team
Teaching/planting
Their life's 'Ways' and 'Means'

Sister Vivian organizer/served chair
Fighter of /Fair/
A scientist who informs/shares/cares
We're so glad she's there

A 'lot' of land
Infusing the arts
Music fills the air
Poetry/Speakers/Dancers
Quite an affair

Local Culinary school Connection
Collaborations/Celebrations

An entrepreneur Extraordinaire

Take a look !
Writer/Children Books/
Natural Lotions /Potions
Flower arrangements/ Entertainment

Kim's (oils)... Herb' N Spice
Makes air smell
healthy/nice

Passionate !
Atty Jillian represents /gives support
and Info
Keeping our Farmers in
the know
traveling cross country
always on the go

Parents/Community Supporters / Partners
Make the 'we'
in unity

A shout or two
May not do
A round-roaring applause
For those of the cause
Who write 'A Lot' of land
By taking a Stand

The Rosa Parks Farmers Market

☼

NORTHEAST FARMERS OF COLOR

Northeast US

Our Vision is to Advance Land Sovereignty in the northeast region through reclamation of permanent and secure land tenure with and for Indigenous, Black, Latinx, and Asian farmers and land stewards who will tend the land in a sacred manner that honors our ancestors' dreams for responsible farming, sustainable human habitat, reintegration of ceremony, restoration of native ecosystems, and global Indigenous cultural preservation.

Poets:
-WILDSEED Community Farm & Healing Village—Naima Penniman
-NEFOC—Hyperion Çaca Yvaire and Stephanie Morningstar

Photos and essay by Stephanie Morningstar
Interwoven Conversation: Hyperion Çaca Yvaire and JuPong Lin

Introduction by Stephanie Morningstar

Plants are magic. They transform light and water into substances that nourish humans, non-humans, and the land. When we eat, we are embodying the alchemical processes of braided stories hidden inside the genomes of seeds, little packets that carry the original instructions of Creation to do what they do best- Create.

Plants are rhythmic beings. They are the dancers to the drummers of Creation. They follow the rhythms and cycles of the earth and the rest of the cosmos- sending down roots when the moon is dark and sending up shoots when she's full.

Humans and non-humans are, by extension, plants. We dance to the same drums and receive the nourishment and healing they provide, therefore ensuring that their part of the covenant they've made with Creation is maintained. By receiving these gifts from our elder siblings, the plants, we inherit that covenant to nurture and heal.

Our story as human beings is a story of seeds and mycorrhizae- of encoded potential and intergenerational, interdenpendent relationship. The story of humankind is written in seedsong, in the prayers for growth and nourishment, the weeps and wails of grief at the ruins we've created, and the re-story-ing of our relationships while we teeter on the verge of the Sixth mass extinction.

To understand foodways is to understand the tipping point of where it all went wrong. Where we fucked up. Where we forgot- and then to remember.

To understand foodways is to understand food's way: the original instructions encoded into seed, land, and kin- the *why* of all of it, the agency and potential of Land and non-human kin, independent of human beings' existence- the intangible, implicit aspects of nature and culture.

To understand foodways is to resituate the storytellers as story*makers*, weaving together our place-thought[1] of geography, history, and cosmology for the purpose of adapting to and co-creating a new set of inherent roles and responsibilities that restores and re-stories the land and our relationships with each other.

The Northeast Farmers of Color Land Trust was co-created to address the deep-time relationships we have with the land, each other, and the Universal Truth, as Kanien'kehá:ka (Mohawk) elder Sakokwenionkwas (Tom Porter) puts it, of our small, young role in relation to Creation. We planted this seed as a direct response, a resistance, to the forgetting, the disconnection, and the hierarchy imposed by Western actors, settler-colonialism, and the momentary yet intense disruptive harm capitalism has wrought on the land, and by extension, the People and non-human kin of the land.

Our vision is simple, yet equally complex: to advance land sovereignty in the Northeast region of Turtle Island in the unceded territories of sovereign nations through reconnection, rematriation, reparations, and stewardship through permanent and secure land tenure with and for Black, Indigenous, Latinx, Asian, and other land stewards of color in a sacred manner that honors our ancestors' collective dreams- for responsible farming, sustainable human habitat, (re)integration of ceremony, re-story-ation of native species ecosystems, and global Indigenous cultural preservation.

We are both/and, a non-binary evolution of the potential of what land trusts are capable of in the Anthropocene. A land trust built by the communities we belong to and are accountable to- the cross-cultural myriad of ancestral relationships we hold like precious embers, weaving our love for kin in each seed we plant, each word we speak, each small patch of earth we reinoculate with mycorrhizae.

1 Vanessa Watts-Powless, in her piece "Indigenous place-thought & agency amongst humans and non-humans (First Woman and Sky Woman go on a European world tour!)" (2013) offers the origins of the term "place-thought" from the teachings of the Anishinaabe creation story known as the "Seven Fires of Creation". She states, "the Fifth Fire, Gizhe-Mnidoo (the Creator) placed his/her thoughts into seeds. In the Sixth Fire, Gizhe-Mnidoo created First Woman (Earth), a place where these seeds could root and grow." (p. 21.)

As Michelle Obama once stated, "when they go low, we go high."[2]
When they speak of "deals", we speak of relationships.
When they affirm "ownership", we affirm stewardship.
When they hoard land-based wealth, we redistribute it.
When they speak of us in the past tense, we dance until the land
remembers us.

In 2019, when we planted this tender seed, there were less than 25
member farms and less than 100 members in our network. A short 3
years later and we have multiplied- our members growing fivefold and
our member farms and cross-cultural land-based projects hiving off into
beautiful expressions of land relationship inoculating the territories they
live and grow on with the same love and care.

We are proud and humbled to pick up the responsibilities of land
stewardship our ancestors tasked us with and are stepping into this role
with care while bearing the expectations and urgency of the communities
who envisioned and called us into being. Because we love the land, and
we love our kin, we are working from the spirit of the Good Mind,
rooted in *ubuntu*, moving slowly, intentionally, asking ourselves what
trappings of colonialism need decentering as we go.

We are not a simple, cookie cutter, status quo land trust founded on
colonial law that sees land as a "resource" meant to extract from,
commodify, or quantify in mere "revenue". Similarly, we approach
conservation as deeply relational and rooted in our original instructions.
Because of this, we are forming a hybrid land trust that is dissolving the
barriers between agriculture and conservation, reconnecting humans as
land stewards and calling upon global Indigenous Knowledge as the best
practice to ensuring food sovereignty, biodiversity, climate resilience, and
community care.

---

2 The White House, Office of the First Lady. (2016, July 25). Remarks by
the first lady at the Democratic National Convention. National Archives and
Records Administration. Retrieved from https://obamawhitehouse.archives.
gov/the-press-office/2016/07/25/remarks-first-lady-democratic-national-
convention

We are a tender, young sapling now, just unfurling our first delicate leaves to receive nourishment from our brother the Sun. We are beginning to transform the light of our community of supporters, our extended relatives, into the nourishment needed to grow big, strong, flexible, and deeply rooted. As we begin to co-create the first of what will be many ceremonies to celebrate the enfoldment of land into our care, we will remember the teachings of the cattail, known in Kanienkeha as onó:ta, which translates to "wraps humans in her gifts." We will wrap our kin in our gifts, our balm of protection. By offering holistic, wrap-around "services" (moreso, acts of love) to the communities we're responding to, we're able to create the interdependent, fractal, iterative, decolonial approach to land relationship that doesn't merely offer business planning, soil mapping, and easements but an ancestrally-rooted, co-creative approach that is emerging as a Venn diagram of programs centering the values we're aligned with and responsible for holding sacred: life-affirming values that are the "go high" response to "go low" settler colonial violence written over the surface of these lands.

The Northeast Farmers of Color Land Trust is a love letter to our ancestors and future generations, a song quietly sung to the land that *we remember*. We remember a time when we were all connected, when we were not separate or above, but equal to and responsible for our role in our short times on this long-lived Earth. As our network of ancestrally-rooted land care begins to extend throughout the territories of the Northeast, our greatest hope and desire is to spark that remembering in others. We take care of the land, and the land takes care of us. Simple, right?

Hyperion Çaca Yvaire and JuPong Lin in Conversation about Tensions in Land Conservation

Hyperion Çaca Yvaire:
I can describe many of the diverse perspectives that seem to be present when it comes to the land trust arena and the land trust endeavor. I should first preface with the understanding that in this given moment, we are all of us gathered here in Turtle Island, are dealing with different inherited strategies for survival under colonial and colonial oppression. And I think that these different strategies persist because they are inevitably grounded in some sort of relationship with land. And sometimes these different relationships and the means by which these strategies do persist, can come into conflict with one another, which causes certain strife or a lot of perceived systemic and psychic violences, and some distinct spiritual and material abuses. Ultimately, there's some resonance in what persists and between what persists and and what materializes. And so we can see in contemporary Land Trust projects some of these different strategies materialize and we can understand them to be the continuation of thinking that comes from the European continent, that has been transformed through, I would say, The Settler Culture of the America's, the United States. So America, United States, Marxism, are in a sense, European phenomena.

JuPong Lin:
Most land trusts protect properties. And the piece of property has boundaries, just like a lawn and within those boundaries, the land is protected. Or maybe we could say, certain kinds of relationships with land are protected. And so in a way that is always going to be provisional, a provisional justice. This is what we got, these are the tools we got in this moment within this settler colonial, capitalist nation state. And I think maybe one of the things we're trying to do in this book, is to fray the boundaries and also start kind of opening up and looking at the connections between these bounded places, to look at plants and organisms…they don't follow property lines.

Hyperion Çaca Yvaire:
LandBack is, even the conversation, it's a very human-focused conversation. Land back says, like, you human stole this land from

me, I own the land, rather than I belong to the land, land and I are deeply, deeply intertwined. Like, I cannot be if this land were not. That sentiment is a symptom of the colonial Zeitgeist. And it's very hard to return land to an indigenous community that seeks to be in a more intimate relationship with that land, a land that is traditionally known to them through settler colonial channels. A title has to be passed, a deed has to be filed, or maybe it's reversed. But it continues a privileging of the human in hierarchical relationship with the land.

JuPong Lin:
I'm thinking of the tensions between different perspectives that this anthology is going to hold, and I always struggle with how to fruitfully navigate those tensions. How do we confront these tensions? How have you done so in your work?

Hyperion Çaca Yvaire:
Your question just pulls me back to my ground. It suggests to me that there's a different way. Because I also experience a great deal of joy when I encounter other things (that repulse me). I speak as a poet for Northeast Farmers of Color Land Trust— it is one of the hats I'm wearing right now. We currently do not possess land, we do not have land that we are the owners of. And yet I'm still capable, and if anything adamant about my piece contributing to this book, when we're talking about relationships with land, and particularly, perhaps even challenging understandings of what the land trust does.

For me, the way in which I have navigated these tensions, is recognizing these tensions to be material, a particular type of material. And that material can be manipulated, as you know, what artists do. And I think it's a material that I like to tie into knots, because when I think about this material, sort of like a string, it's fibrous, it's a fiber, good tension. And these knots allow us to create these networks; we can stand upon these knots. And there's something about the weight that we can apply to the mass consciousness that can be directed onto that knot that allows something to push through that fabric, allows us to puncture holes in that fabric. And it's okay for things to be tattered. All things need to come to an end which is a really good phrase to hold on to.

JuPong Lin:
What a wonderful metaphor knots. I'm a knitter, so in knitting, we talk
a lot about tension. Tension is needed, a certain amount of tension is
needed to create a fabric. And the skill is in maintaining the right amount
of tension with certain kinds of fiber to make certain kinds of fabric.

Hyperion Çaca Yvaire:
To continue with the the tension, the fabric, the knitting, I think it's
important to understand that many land trusts can be understood to
be forms of cultural ecosystem structures or cultural ecosystem service
providers. They have a responsibility to conserve, protect, sustain a given
piece of territory. And they have to install themselves administratively,
and develop a culture that allows access and allows the administration to
be sustained.

Iontó:rats (Hunter)
by Stephanie Morningstar

tracing inky serpentine ashphalt
sliced though a stand of secondary growth
kárha
forest
where the remnants of elders
still receive love and care
from a network of earthen neurons
that resist any shape but their own

silver shock of eyeshine, of teardrop tail
jolt my ever-deepening memory
of wildness surrounding me
wildness still in me
in my sleep, tangling branches entwine my hair
fruiting bodies bloom from my breast

crumpled and lifeless
the body of your sister lies discarded
on a roadside too steep to sweep clean
her torso carelessly strewn over burm
a ditch dug for the comfort of others

her delicate frame
tangled in mud and low brush,
never claimed as prize
her body will not wrap around
the tiny wrists of our newborns
ceasing generations of seed yet born
a ceremony never put through

you dart away from my million-candle power beam
springing forth into wood dense with cold
under a moon half illuminated
and half dark with mystery

straining to catch a glimpse of your majesty
attempting a count of your starry points
seeing nothing but you
dancing
away from the unnatural shape of my vessel,
my bright eyes shining, matching yours

You leap lest you become transfixed
with a heart pounding
with instinctual fear and no reason to trust
weak, fluorescent orange-clad men
who have no intention of looking you in the eye
or feeling your spirit's truth
men who look like the wood you live in
who you smell before you see
with your wizened eye

if I were to hunt you
it would not be with the force of fire
or weapons of war
made mad by hoarding
eating so much that it chokes
it would not be with rubber shielding my feet
from the cold damp earth
that your hooves call home

if I were to hunt you
it would not be with anything made
by the hands of the men
who have forgotten
their names
their responsibilities
that they are a part of everything
that they, too, are *otsistohkwa'shon:a*
made of stars

if I were to hunt you
I would honor you as kin

dancing through moss, trees,
lichen-rich rocks
wild eye meeting my own
wild heart beating like my own
Shonkwaia'tison's breath escaping us
silvering the night air
meeting betwixt the sharp coldness
of the silent dark night

if I were to hunt you
I would walk low and firm to
Iethi'nistenha ohontsia
Mother earth
making no sound with my foot
I would plant myself deep in the soil
and root in as a tree that has seen more moons
than any of our ancestors can recall

if I were to hunt you
I would draw back my arrow
on bowstring taut and worn shiny
from many other nights such as this

prayers silently whisper-sung
you turn to offer me
clean aim at your heart
beating as fast as mine

asking permission
a sacred contract
an original instruction
a universal truth

obsidian-sharp, point ringing true
with mercy and thanks
kneeling in our resting places

the face of death is not for the meek

or the kept, or the weak
to meet that eye, once so wild
now wise with the knowing
what you are seeing now is
the last thing you will ever see
in this life

last breaths and electric remnants
your sacred vessel lays bent beneath me
in silent honoring

Niawenhkó:wa
great thanks

know this *Oskenón:ton*
Deer Spirit:

You feed my family
as the high summer grass fed yours

Your skins will clothe me as they clothed you
Your bone will sing alive again
under the moon
on a drum made from Your soft belly

our dance will be remembered
sitting by fire
under stars in the cold night air
under a low-slung slice of silvery moon
Iethi'sotha ahsonthehnehkha karahkwa
our grandmother
who pulls the tides
governs the planting
links our sovereign bodies

your memory and spirit
will be thanked and lauded
as the Kin you are

the One who was sung into Skyworld
on a path of *niiohontésha*
the first and last fruit
mottled with stars

Ó:nen wa'tekhenonwerá:ton ne tyonhéhkwen
now I have thanked the food/sustenance

akwé:kon énska entitewahwe'nón:ni ne onkwa'nikòn:ra tánon Teiethinonhwerá:ton ne Kontírio tsi tkonhtká:was ne oià:ta, ohwísha, Óstien, Órwhare, Onekwénsha.
all one we will wrap it up of our minds and we greet, thank, and acknowledge the animals that they give up for us their body, energy, bone, fur, blood.

Tho ká:ti naióhton nonkwa'nikòn:ra.
Let our minds be that way.

If I were to hunt you,
this is the way I would do the deed
honoring you
for the untamed heart
and untamed blood
that beats within
your stag-strong soul.

A Coalition of Storms
by Hyperion Çaca Yvaire

I cut my teeth yesterday,
but I track the motions.
No blueblood charity is gonna
grow us wings,
No centuries of underland utopia is digging us a way out,
any time soon.

I know visioning the power
in a blacker nature
won't disappear the dams.

Bound or unbound,
in their own special and hungry visage
someone like me rubs too often against the grains,
but for me deep disorder is grounding at midnight
and I tell you now,
there's no secret rhythm for making kin;
the best beat is always situated.

Inara slammed her hand down.
Like the pink bear addressing a blue sky,
her palm settled atop a hemlock stump,
rattling the gammas around
the Microcosmic Lichen Café

she whispered to us "there is an ancestry that sours your lemonade!"

She reminds me of the
danger Socrates met.

But what can be done?

I have big human feet and
practicing the Lambada is easier than
crossing strange unkindnesses in the grasses.
While we sort through what a zoo-break could do
for her on my hip, this earthly education
quietly spirals towards
the place where fairies make respite.
It's necessary to make coalitions out of thunderstorms,
how else would you parent?

Unyielding- but bent as hart's neck
sipping microplastics at the fjord-
the spirit is scattered like too many islands... {in} {dis} {tinc} {t}

in a settled and murderous colonial disregard.

Each fragment holds
stories of a thousand new folkways in need
of a national beer,
but they won't survive rearranging the edges of the Horizon,
Papu.

They can hack and hack away
at a billion personal histories,
reaching beyond the canvas,
scrambling for lost languages
Perhaps leaving the many bales of turtles displeased-
But my diaphragm only calms near water
and my lungs only fill
when there's shade.

The matter is clearer whenever a storm visits.

The Day of the Slip-away Salt Water
by Hyperion Çaca Yvaire

Near the Hudson,
Sitting with Foolish
I called on my great,
great, great, granddaughter to guide me-

the scene that swooshed onto me after silencing
Foolish upon the shore
was a wild rendition of "Tropical Mountain
visits Sleeping Bear"
by the playwright Salisphere Mantle,
in its 24th Act— the moment when the Scorpion-Man Elder delivers his
13-step emotional appeal
in service of the season changes
and commemorating the Day of the Slip-a-way Salt water.
 Gladly,
I swooned to the turtle shells a-cink-a-cink-a-cink-a- cink,
all those beads of sap rattling around, dancing with the ghost of _____.
Hard to miss a beat when you've got 8 arms, they always say.

Gratefully,
I was awakened with the sweet breath of the flutist
And felt myself falling in bliss into the breeze and into the throaty call of
the heron— Is this land or a landing, they wondered to me.

Then I felt the pull of the stag's tongue lapping me up
Unsubmerging me from the floodsong.

There was Foolish again, and with troubled spirit
they said to me "I own this land,"
To which I sang "and you will give it back."

Hyperion Çaca Yvaire: Land and Justice as a Body
(an excerpt from a conversation with JuPong Lin)

One of the things that is very interesting about the use of justice as a system, is the metaphor of the body—that justice is a body that in the way of other bodies, has to be cared for, particularly the earthly body. When we refer to justice or multispecies jurisprudence, we're trying to articulate that there is no nature beyond what is part of nature, that we are nature as well. So like earthiness, the body of the Earth, the planetary understanding there, justice is part of that planetary understanding. And it is like anything, any other part of the planet, it needs care.

I often wonder, what would it look like if we could intervene in the conversation around land back and really introduce multispecies jurisprudence, really talk about that? Like, let's change the language, right here, the idea that we need to be inclusive and more conscious and repair. Let's make sure that the intention can be made material through careful, action, precise, careful action.

If justice is a system, or perhaps multiple systems, I think that's appropriate when we refer to nation states. Each nation state has its own perspective on what justice is, and in situations or matters that are planetary, such as climate change, there are multiple nation state oriented systems of justice, multiple national, corporate, industrial systems of making food or making a way for food, as opposed to ensuring food has its way. Instead, the type of systems that I want to ground my thinking on are planetary systems.

I want to really ground in our bodies again, and ground in an understanding that allows for the possibility that justice is a body, that it has multiple systems within it. And that these systems are increasingly dependent and reliant upon each other. And that when we can identify/ diagnose what it needs, what other bodies we need to bring into us, or what other spirits we need to have congress with. When we pay attention to how the body of justice is functioning, we can diagnose the types of justice phenomena such as the recent gun shootings—the racist violence on children, domestic violence, environmental degradation, redlining, all of these things. We should not just point to injustices and lose sight of their interconnections with land. Social ills are in fact, the endocrine system of a body. And that we can't just remove that one piece, because everything is connected. We have to work on everything: we have to go through a diet; we need to be sure that we are hydrating; that we are exercising; that we are practicing in a manner that seeks to realize an improvement upon our condition.

WILDSEED Community Farm & Healing Village

WILDSEED
by Naima Penniman

636 Rudd Pond Road
once a single family home
became a sanctuary
for thousands
of bodies
a thousand shades
of earth

we painted the house like the sun
plastered the walls with clay
transformed the shelves
into apothecary
library
altar

the same house where
a dozen Pilipino womxn lay down across the floor
journeying with their ancestors in a circle of light

the same floor where
the djembes erupted
laced with liberation lyrics
ignited by young Black fire

and we strung waist beads with
grrrls on the cusp on womxnhood

and held ceremony
concocted medicine
harbored our elders

and cooked food for family
on their way back from penitentiary visits

with loved ones locked far far away
beside the pond that became a shrine for Osun
where a Muslim father buried his son's placenta
and a pagan mother got married to herself
the same pond where
we traced a labyrinth in the snow when it froze over

where we learned how to make our own remedies
from the plants growing wild around us

the soil became the ground in which to plant our wildest dreams
where we poured libation
scattered ashes
practiced magic

where we grew Lenape blue corn
and sugar baby watermelons
boiled maple water into syrup
where we stretched our imaginations
remembered our sweetness

the land that was once a single family's backyard
transformed into training grounds
community classrooms
childcare spaces
political art tents
a freedom playground for Black trans humans
a space to breathe

the same land that taught us
about slowing down
to feel everything
about generosity of spirit
about defending what we love
about not giving up

the water that listened to our tears
while the beavers slapped their tails and the big turtle swam

where we shaped vessels out of creek clay
floated baskets made of leaves
filled with flower pedal offerings

the same water that taught us about change
tracing the mountains that taught us about permanence

the same mountains where 18 teenagers climbed together
with their intentions tucked in their pockets
where every single one, not without struggle, made it to the summit
and we lay our deep-breathing bodies on the sun-warmed rocks
that pressed us up against the sky
pledging our pumping hearts to life

the same sky that changed colors
spanning the wide open horizon
never had we seen so many stars
never so many chances to make a wish
as they streaked across the blackness

the big dome sky that taught us
we are part
of something so much bigger
so small, so significant
we are
no accident

and we are never alone

636 Rudd Pond Road
a sanctuary for thousands
once a single family home

☼

Precious
by Naima Penniman

I want to listen
to the deep
water inside you
attend to all it remembers
and satisfy the thirst
that has gone on way too long

you deserve water
delivered to the shore of your lips
dripping down to your heart

you deserve love
the kind that patiently
melts over the flickers of you
that survived annihilation

stoke the embers
offer cedar
to the last coals still aglow
induce a spiral plume
of tree sap crackle
smoke becoming ceremony
in a time of too much choking

you deserve oxygen
the gasp of breath
expanding the space around you
that never ending room for you
that dark matter
that you matter
to the galactic tapestry
as vast as this universe is wide

you deserve time

I want to spin you a cocoon
shimmering and safe
a sturdy capsule
suspended at the edge of it all

where you can dissolve all you want
let go of all you need to
do nothing but dream
your way
into a whole new state
of being

you deserve flight

you deserve soar

you deserve to be carried
on the wind

and held in the calm

I want to cradle you
into my chest
like the most precious pulsing song

I want to listen
to the deep
water inside you
attend to all it remembers
and satisfy the thirst
that has gone on way too long

you deserve water

☼

JuPong Lin and Hyperion Çaca Yvaire in Conversation about Spirituality and Kinmaking

JuPong Lin:
There's a form of any religion that is dogmatic that exacerbates the disconnection with land, exacerbates social ills. But every religion also has a mystical strand, and teachings about the interconnectedness of different systems.

Hyperion Çaca Yvaire:
I feel that a mystical practice that comes from any religious background or spiritual condition is one that seeks to gain an understanding of relation that is not bound by rules, not just rote, not bound by fear of spiritual expansion. I think that mysticism seeks to expand and develop relationships. And I think that there are particular dogmas that seek to reduce and sustain particular relationships. And there are tensions there, and perhaps the planet is actually bringing us to a space where those tensions can be turned into really viable knots and something can be done with them. It seems like we haven't had the opportunity to encounter that yet, to really see what happens when we put mystics in a room with dogmatics, when they're given a real situation such as a great famine due to poor land management.

My practice is as a Cosmo-ecological being that is committed to Cosmoecological service, a being does not breathe air, they breathe chaos. When they inhale, this chaos, they can choose to exhale some form of harmony that is best at that given time. And I think it is interesting to think that this group of poets through their investigation and relationship-making with the land—Kinmaking—they are in some way, being gathered into a textual Congress to fray or fragment a particular understanding that causes harm, you know, to fragment and fray a particular understanding that sees itself as supreme.

JuPong Lin:
On the note of Kinmaking. Maybe we can close with a couple of thoughts about Kinmaking. I want to bring in the work of Kim Tall Bear who wrote in "The US-Dakota War and Failed Settler Kinship" (2021) that "'making kin' can help forge relations between Peoples in ways that

produce mutual obligation instead of settler-colonial violence upon which the US continues to build itself." It's not easy being kin.

Hyperion Çaca Yvaire:
Yeah, exactly. It is not easy being kin. But it's fulfilling. It's life affirming being kin. That's the difference. It is life affirming being kin. The distinction between representation and reproduction, the recognition that food has a way, and, you know, we should get out of its way, that there's this congress of beings that we bring into our body that has their own art. We spoke about justice as a body, to understand the body of justice as one with which we make kin.

Photo (opposite): Buffalo by James Calvin Schaap

PART II: THE ARTS FOODWAYS, COMMUNITIES, AND CONSERVED LANDS

Poetry and Breath by Hyperion Çaca Yvaire
(excert from a conversation with JuPong Lin)

I think there's something fascinating about poetry being historically, a very strong spoken form, you know, that it is this we take in, we take in this with our breath. We are breathing chaos, at any given point in time, we take in this chaos from all of these different chemicals and all these different beings breathing out, we hold it in our bodies for a moment, and then we choose to release it in a way that produces a different sonic wave. And that we may do this unintentionally without too much understanding. But as a poet, you are practicing this doing, you are taking in things through your experience, your encounter, but also when you breathe and you release your poetry, you are transmuting. I'm getting emotional, because, I don't have the opportunity or many spaces to talk about food as having a way of its own. Imagine what would happen how much connection we might reproduce, yes, how much empathy we might experience, if we build spaces in which we can talk about food having a way of its own. Hopefully this book contributes to that.

Artwork: Winds of Change by Judy Thompson

POETRY X HUNGER

Artwork by Diane Wilbon Parks

Maryland

"Fighting Hunger One Poem at a Time"— Poet Willeena Booker

Essayist:
-Hiram Larew, Ph.D.

Poets:
-Willeena Booker
-John L. Dutton II
-Dianna L. Grayer, Ph.D.
-Antoni Ooto

Poetry X Hunger:
Lessons Learned from an Anti-Hunger Initiative
by Hiram Larew, Ph.D.

Poetry about Hunger

A few years ago, a search for hunger-related poetry would have come up nearly empty-handed. Yes, many, many poems have been composed over the years about hunger of the heart, spirit and soul. But until recently, not many were available about hunger of the stomach.

This in spite of the fact that poetry has been useful in raising the public's attention about a variety of other social causes such as racial inequality, homelessness, poverty, environmental concerns, and the like. For example, Emma Lazarus's *The New Colossus* at the base of the Statue of Liberty, remains a clarion and motivational call about America's welcoming approach to immigrants and immigration.

I launched *Poetry X Hunger* in 2018 to make sure that poetry was included in the anti-hunger toolkit. I roused poets to write about hunger and the response has been remarkable. Nearly 300 poems and counting from a diversity of poets from around the world are now posted on the *Poetry X Hunger* website. Clearly, if asked to bring their talents to a worthy cause such as hunger or land care, poets will respond.

Poems posted on *Poetry X Hunger*, a few of which are showcased in this section, explore all aspects and facets of hunger, from its history to its causes, to its impacts and haunt. Malnutrition, food waste and, paradoxically, obesity (often linked to poor quality food) are covered as well. In other words, the "focus" of hunger poems is very broad.

longing for more
by Willeena Booker

barebones palette salivating on stale air
inhale aromatic memories before cupboards were left bare

praying for a meal but a morsel is barely there
silent duel with hunger's boastful stare

one country wallows in gluttony yet another laments in despair
if all men are created equal why is life so unfair

incessant gnawing deep in the pit of my pitiful soul
longing for sustenance to overflow an empty bowl

mocking me, looming large, whither I go
trembling hands unmask pain, my desperation grows

head tucked low veiling the shame
begging for food, oh God, this is insane!

the Earth is the Lord's and the fullness thereof
starvation is a poison, the antidote is love

full bellies pass by in quick paced steps
failing to see my hour of woe and regret

God bless the one who grows his own
tilling the ground with hands of his native home

villagers pledge to restore the land
plant more trees united we stand

hunger, a silent pandemic raging out of control
millions go hungry, but who keeps tally of the toll

swaddled skeletons and emaciated remains
hidden 6 feet deep, the world in motion yet unchanged

come stand with me, brothers and sisters, let us rise as one
act to eradicate hunger until global victory is won

Photo: Hospers Elevator by Joanne Alberda

All forms of poetry have also been showcased on the *Poetry X Hunger* website, from traditional forms to free verse. This variety has been showcased so that anti-hunger leaders will find at least one poem, maybe more that suits their needs.

Importantly, the power of poetry to Speak Up depends upon a huge range of contributing voices from a wide diversity of races and cultures using many, many modes of expression. Poetry's prismatic array makes it potent. In fact, ensuring that we move beyond a solo or monochromatic voice to a chorus of talents is a key to *Poetry X Hunger's* success. Poems from a single culture fall short.

Poetry X Hunger has deliberately reached out to and showcased poets from rural, suburban and inner-city/urban settings, from schools, campuses, reservations, and senior centers, and from Australia to Zimbabwe and many points in between.

And, in addition to posting a poem's text, we've posted recordings of poets presenting their poems in their fine voices so that differently-abled visitors are offered options for enjoying the poems. These recording are proving useful in allowing users to fully interpret and savor the poems. Recordings are also easily useful for playback at online meetings.

There is always more work to do to enhance diversity and accessibility. For example, one of *Poetry X Hunger's* goal is to offer poems in various languages; currently most all of the poems are in English with a few in Spanish and one in Cheyenne. Presenting multi-lingual offerings is a goal. And, while there are poems by notable as well as less-well-known poets on the website, we'd love to include more work by young poets as a way of deepening *Poetry X Hunger's* impact on anti-hunger work in the years and decades to come. We're also working to include recordings of poems that are presented using American Sign Language.

Yes, intentionally enlisting poetry from a wide range of backgrounds and perspectives is a key step to building wide buy-in, promoting fairness, reflecting myriad views and, encouraging participatory commitment to the cause, be it hunger or land trusts.

As *Poetry X Hunger* was getting off the ground, some wonderful opportunities arose to partner with key stakeholders. For example, the United Nations Food and Agriculture Organization's (UNFAO) office in Washington, DC, USA expressed interest in including poetry in its commemoration of World Food Day (October 16). The result has been a multi-year partnership between *Poetry X Hunger* and UNFAO; we've jointly issued calls for hunger poems for each of the last several years. The partnership has helped us sweeten our interactions with poets because we can promise to showcase selected poems in UNFAO's widely-shared newsletter, and to limelight poems at high-level World Food Day conclaves.

Along the way, the Capital Area Food Bank which is a large food aid distribution center that serves the Greater Washington, DC area has also partnered by hosting a first-ever Food Bank Poet-in-Residence (PiR) in 2020 and 2021. What a concept! The poems that were written by the PiRs have been used by the Food Bank in its messaging. Similarly, the Alliance to Cut Hunger's Hunger Free Communities team has offered the microphone to hunger poets to open or close national anti-hunger meetings. Pennsylvania State University's Global Learning in Agriculture initiative showcases poems from *Poetry X Hunger* as an agricultural classroom teaching tool. We've also received support from the Maryland Arts Councils to develop the *Poetry X Hunger* website. Our other partners include House of Worship, elementary and high school classroom teachers, poetry organizations, community groups and many others. Often one partnership leads to another.

All to say, partners are critically important legitimizers and amplifiers. They help to ensure that poems are put to use. Of course, they can also pitch in by offering honoraria, prizes, and operational support. Perhaps most significantly, they influence us; as each partner brings unique perspectives to bear, *Poetry X Hunger*'s approaches and goals have been refreshed.

Hunger Visited My Classroom
by John L. Dutton II

Hunger visited my classroom every morning during my first year as a teacher.
Though it feels like forever ago, I never forget his blue eyes
Nor his unkempt shaggy, blond hair.
He masqueraded as an eight-year-old boy
Dressed each day in the same ragged, filthy Power Rangers t-shirt.
The rings of dirt around his neck,
And the grime hiding deep under his fingernails
Were his only companions.
His classmates ostracized him,
As they called him Pig Pen after the character in Charlie Brown.
Malnourishment attempted to hide
Behind a mountain of synonyms:
Thin, skinny, underweight, boney, scraggy, scrawny, beanpole -
The list seems endless
Like the hunger creeping continually around this boy's belly.
Hunger tried to stifle me; however, no matter how late his bus arrived,
I always made sure he received his bag of breakfast
Containing French toast sticks with syrup that never stayed contained
As I did my temper toward his constantly sticky desk.
I knew I could never defeat hunger as he grinned at me each morning,
But I could put a dent in him and
Make sure he knew I wasn't going to take it easy on him.
Jolly Ranchers, Life Savers, Sour Balls, and, my personal favorite,
Werther's Original Caramels filled the glass fishbowl on my desk.
I never missed an opportunity to reward any positive action or answer.
I called upon him at every opportunity to help with mundane tasks:
Passing out papers, sweeping the floor, walking papers down the hall to the office.
The smile on that boy's face lit up my heart
As he enjoyed whatever treat I gave him.
On the last day of school, I gave him an entire bag of Jolly Ranchers, his personal favorites.
The following year, Mrs. P, his new teacher, and I greeted Hunger
As he tried to slip silently into school on a brisk September morning.

I handed him an entire bag of Jolly Ranchers, and his smile nearly broke my heart.

As I watched Mrs. P escort him down the hall and into her classroom, I whispered to myself, "Not today, Hunger, not today. Not on my watch."

Here are some *Poetry X Hunger*'s out-of-the-ordinary activities that are relevant to land trusts:

•   **Readings and Workshops** – *Poetry X Hunger* has offered in-person and zoom-based readings in all kinds of venues including Houses of Worship, art galleries, libraries, youth gatherings, wineries, community centers, international hunger meetings, etc. We've also held workshops for teens, community groups and others. And, readings don't end with the last poems; they often lead to new partnerships and to new poetry. We also are encouraging attendees to donate to anti-hunger causes.

•   **Interviews** – *Poetry X Hunger* jumps at any chance to be interviewed in magazines, newspapers, blog hosts, poetry and anti-hunger groups about the role of poetry in Speaking Back to Hunger. We've also flipped the microphone around so that we interview movers and shakers such as Poet Laureates, anti-hunger organizations, and Youth Poetry Leaders and then post those interviews on the website. Of special fun has been our recorded visits with the very creative founders of groups such as AgArts, The Milk House and NatureCulture.

•   **Showcasing Poems** –To make it easy for anti-hunger groups to find a hunger poem, we published and distributed an e-collection of hunger poems and recordings from *Poetry X Hunger*. We haven't yet featured a hunger poem on a billboard or during Superbowl halftime, but give us time!

Feed the Bellies
by Dianna L. Grayer, Ph.D.

The children cry,
Squeals in the day.
Tossing and turning in the night.
Piercing the hearts and souls of their parents.
Who themselves are,
Bewildered, distraught - deprived.
Unable to help their children or themselves.

Kids are hungry.
Without food in this wide wide world of resources.
Empty bellies. Empty spirits.
Enduring pain, ongoing suffering,
A void of nutrients because of lack of resources,
Or the lack of consciousness and compassion?

The children cry because of waste.
Insensitivity and selfishness.
A lack of care.
When buckets of fruit drop and left to rot.
When vegetables overgrow and tossed away.
When tons of food decay in our stores and factories.
When we take more than we can chew.
And scrape the rest down the drain or in the garbage.

Stop wasting food when the young bellies hurt.
The earth's bounty delivers enough for us all.
There's an abundance of food in this wide wide world.
Share the resources.
Nourish the innocent souls.
Let them survive and thrive- so they can rise.
Grow it -can it -dry it -and ship it.
Lives depends on it.
With compassion, empathy and consciousness,
We can quell the hungry cries.
Feed the bellies. Feed the people.

• **Residencies and Appearances** – As mentioned, *Poetry X Hunger* has arranged one-to-two-day poetry residencies for poets at food banks. Beyond that, we're in the process of launching a year-long "residency" for a poet to work with a county's Food Bank. We're confident that this long-term relationship will lead to all kinds of exciting outcomes. We've also facilitated many, many appearances – live, online, recorded, etc. — of poets at anti-hunger conclaves. We're finding that as more poets present their work, more are invited to do so.

• **Helping Teachers** – In consultation with *Poetry X Hunger*, colleagues at Pennsylvania State University have developed a "Here's How to Bring Poetry into Your Food-Focused Classes" teaching module and curriculum for use by K-18 teachers. The *Poetry X Hunger* website is listed in the module as a key resource. Teachers are "eating it up" – they love the idea of using poetry to surprise and engage students as topics like hunger, agriculture, food are discussed in classes and workshops.

Of course, poetry is only one of the Arts. *Poetry X Hunger* is often called upon to draw in other kinds of artists to the anti-hunger cause. Embracing other expressive forms provides countless opportunities. Just imagine, for example, a choreographed dance that interprets a poem titled, *Hunger's Haunt*. Or, a set of storytelling tales that center on food waste. Surely, poetry can be integrated seamlessly and powerfully within a video or musical artist's work about hunger. And here's the thing: If done mindfully, such extensions of *Poetry X Hunger's* focus don't need to fuzz its mandate or bog things down. Such artistic collaborations strengthen the message rather than detract from it. Having said all of that, we've found that it's important to provide a safe and near sacred place that values and showcases hunger poetry alone. And so, finding a balance that maintains poetry as a focal point while enriching that work with other art forms can be daunting, gratifying, innovative and challenging.

With *Poetry X Hunger's* greater visibility has come some turning point decisions. For example, we've been asked by anti-hunger organizations if we would let them find very famous people to present our website's poems in fundraising campaigns. This kind of amplification could be amazingly effective in sharing hunger poems with the general public. At the same time, issues arise like ownership of copyright, payment to poets and creative control of the poem's presentation. The pros and cons of "going big-time" certainly need to be considered carefully before diving in.

Perhaps the most challenging opportunity is to plan for the future when the present moment claims so much of our time. We often don't have the chance or even see the need to consider what an initiative like *Poetry X Hunger* should become in five or ten years. More importantly, we often fail to build the buy-in or capacity that's needed to transition and hand-off leadership when such changes come. And also, with *Poetry X Hunger*, we have valued a very informal model, one that has no bank account, no by-laws, no board (we do have an informal group of advisors who help when needed), and we are not registered as a non-profit. To be honest, during the initiative's tender early years, this informality has been wonderfully enabling in its flexibility. And hey, as a poetry initiative, such organic, creative informality has seemed pretty appropriate! Moving forward, however, there will likely come a time when more formal structures, processes and strategies will become necessary.

Perhaps the most valuable take-away of all is this: Poetry is an uncommon, rarely used tool in some important take-up-the-cause toolkits. As we work to advance changes that are needed on policy, cultural and behavioral fronts, we'll want to continue to learn all that we can about the best ways to tap into Poetry's Power and Magic.

Ribbons in Your Field
by Antoni Ooto

no matter how much rain falls
you will be all right

recall spring
where nature whispers to a waiting field

where all hopes faithfully soak
nudging a belief in growth and change

leaning forward
in peace   sowing trust

like a monk dropping seed
blessing its fairness

seasoning a waiting field
while keeping that final vow

Photo: Peru Market by Janine Calsbeek

AGARTS

Iowa

Mission:

AgArts imagines and promotes healthy food systems through the arts. A young non-profit, we've worked with artists throughout the United States and abroad to reframe and open a discussion of what agriculture can do to enhance a healthy population on a more sustainable planet. Through our work, we have opened channels of communication that have drawn audiences into new ideas and perspectives about the food they eat, how it is produced, and how it affects our culture and well-being.

Essayist and Photographer:
                    -Dr. Mary Swander

AgArts: Strange Bedfellows Join Forces for a Regenerative Future
by Mary Swander

Overview:
An Old Order Amish grandpa peers into the AgArts window in our store front office in downtown Kalona, Iowa, his long white beard brushing against the glass. His hand up to his eyes, he peers at our poster about AgArts farm residencies and an announcement about our latest podcast. Inside, I am working at my desk, emailing an oral historian and audio artist who will be arriving soon from North Carolina to document a Guatemalan community garden in Northeast Iowa. The audio artist will be in residence on a nearby AgArts-connected farm a mile from the Mississippi River.

Soon, I slip into my recording booth to interview a writer, Fulbright scholar and permaculture expert on the rejuvenation of her farm south of Calcutta, India. She details how she designed her landscape and built up the soil to make her farm more productive financially and ecologically, becoming a draw for fish and wildlife.

So goes a day in the life of the executive director of AgArts, a non-profit that works at the intersection of arts and agriculture. We are based in Amishland where sustainability is modeled, but we reach out to artists and farmers throughout the world to join together to work for a more regenerative agricultural future.

Organizational Structure:
AgArts maintains a board of directors and an advisory board. We operate with an executive director, a podcast producer, a webmaster, a manager, interns and volunteers.

Background:
Ten years ago, I stood on the stage of the Chestnut Center of the Arts, a repertoire theatre in Marshfield, WI, engaged in a talk-back after a performance of my play Farmscape. I had written the drama with my students in a class I taught at Iowa State University. I thought the play was going to be a class exercise with a life of one semester. My class and

I had collaborated on a verbatim drama, one based on interviews of people engaged in the changing environmental farmscape of Iowa. The students fanned out over the countryside, recording the exact words of large farmers and small, industrial seed sales people, vintners, and B & B owners. We wound their words together, pushing ourselves to end the year with one performance in a black box theatre in the basement of the university student union.

I was relieved that we'd made it that far. The students happily went home for break with good grades. Then the phone rang and Fred Kirschenmann, an ISU colleague, at the Aldo Leopold Center for Sustainable Agriculture was on the phone with a small grant to send me out on the road for three more performances of Farmscape. And I was off. For the next five years, I toured the play to farmers' barns throughout the Midwest, to the USDA in Washington, D.C.

In Wisconsin, the audience was filled with a mixture of "big" and "little" ag. producers who farmed thousands of acres with conventional techniques, to those who were looking for a more regenerative approach. A Monsanto executive shared the stage with me and we both fielded questions, the audience always respectful, but leaning in, to have their voices heard. A lively, but civilized, flow of conversation flooded the room, neighbors and friends agreeing to disagree, their very livelihoods bet on the agricultural methods they were employing.

Back at ISU, I visited with Kirschenmann about the dialogue arising from the Farmscape performances.

"I've had emails from people all over the U.S. telling me that they've changed the whole way they're eating after seeing Farmscape," I said..

"I'm wondering if we couldn't start an organization to encourage more dialogue between the arts and agriculture," Kirschenmann said. "I know they are strange bedfellows, but I think the arts will be what opens our eyes to the subject of agriculture."

We began with a campus group, inviting students and community members from journalism to landscape architecture, from music to

agronomy to participate. Soon, we were hosting guest speakers and giving
out small grants for events as diverse as exhibits of farm women's aprons
to the botanical drawing of George Washington Carver. I left ISU in
2016, took AgArts with me to Kalona, Iowa, applied for 501 (c)3 status
and set up a store front office in 2020.

Photo: Round Bales by Mary Swander

Current Programs:
Once I'd moved to my new location in the middle of the Old Order
Amish settlement, I set up **Farm-to-Artist Residencies**. In this unique
program, farms throughout the U.S. host artists for one week to one
month. The artists get to know the farmers and their agricultural issues,
and their conservation and regenerative practices. The artists then
incorporate this agricultural knowledge into their own creative work, and
within a year of the residency, produce a piece of art that is a reflection
of direct, hands-on experience and observation of farming.

To kick off the program, I brought the Connemara Lads, a traditional Irish duo of flute and accordion from the west coast of Ireland to reside for two weeks on the "east coast" of Iowa. The New Hope Farm is nestled in the Driftless Region of the state—rough, hilly nonglaciated terrain, with a fresh, clear trout stream running through the property. A large vegetable garden, milking cows, sheep, and a friendly dog and cat and an engaging family greeted the Lads.

Mornings were filled with music drifting out of the guest house, washing over the farm and the valley. During their stay, the Lads became familiar not only with diversified farming techniques, but with the philosophy behind New Hope, based on the work of Dorothy Day and Peter Maurin, founders of the Catholic Worker Movement. Worker Farms were established to practice regenerative agriculture, provide hospitality to those in need, and help the poor.

The Lads pulled weeds in the garden with the farmers and brought vegetables and music to the homeless shelter in Dubuque. At the end of their stay, the Lads had composed a tune for the farm and toured around the state of Iowa, performing in Opera Houses, Art Centers, and general stores.

After the Connemara Lads' success, other farms wanted residencies and other artists wanted to visit farms. AgArts now has a network of farms throughout Iowa, Nebraska and New York State. Both artists and farmers apply for this program through our website, discovering our programming through booths at conferences, social media sites, newspaper articles, and word of mouth.

Artists have continued to reside on our farms, including dancers, theatre artists, visual artists, photographers, writers and musicians. They have published poems and articles, videoed dance performances, performed concerts and painted pieces in response to their residencies. The artists have learned about restoring prairie and wetlands, energy conservation, no-till planting, cover crops, food forests, and new models of distribution of products such as CSAs. In return, the farmers have enjoyed the energy of hosting artists and have learned about some of the joys and complexities of the creative arts.

AgArts pays each farmer a stipend for a residency. It pays each artists' room, board and often travel while in residency.

AgArts also produces **AgArts from Horse and Buggy Land**, a bi-monthly, 30-minute podcast that focuses on the Amish, sustainability and the wider rural environment. Buggy Land is available wherever you get your podcasts (Apple, Spotify, etc.) Mary Swander hosts the podcast from a fictional Freemartin Town. She includes monologues of her life among the Amish, storytelling by other farmers, interviews with folk artists and agricultural experts, and accompanying folk, blues, jazz and classical music. Douglas Burns, a well-known state journalist, has called AgArts from Horse & Buggy Land a Prairie Home Companion without the sexual harassment.

Buggy Land raises money through Supercast memberships, and encourages audience participation through contests and call-in comments recorded on Speak Pipe through the website.

Communications:
In addition to the window display and podcast, AgArts connects with the public through **booths and panel presentations** at agricultural and artistic conferences and events.

AgArts **teaches online classes in poetry and non-fiction writing** and **publishes creative writing and artwork** through its online journal *The Blazing Star.*

AgArts maintains an active website (www.agarts.org) where the podcasts are posted, contests are announced, and artist-in-residence projects are displayed. Examples of art projects include:

—Farm Art Zine, by Jean Graham, former coordinator of public art for the city of Austin, TX. A 50-frame downloadable zine documenting her residency on the diversified Geyer farm near Oxford, IA.

—River House on the Prairie, by Annie Chapman Brewer, a French horn musician and teacher, composed a piece for horn and wildlife at Whiterock Conservancy.

—Pie and Tornadoes, by Buzz Masters, Deer Isle, Maine, visual artist and gallery owner, published in Creative Maine—an article and painting.

AgArts also cultivates an audience on social media, including sites on Facebook Instagram, and Twitter. It sends special announcements on an email newsletter.

AgArts has been interviewed and profiled on local media, public and community radio stations, and on national podcasts.

Affiliations:
Central College in Pella, Iowa, partners with AgArts to provide a hands-on learning experience for its students. Central has sent interns to AgArts to help with grant writing and advertising copy, newsletters, and podcast commentary. Interns have also staffed conference booths and performance sites.

I have given talks and workshops on AgArts for the ISU Sustainable Agricultural Program, Practical Farmers of Iowa and The Center for Rural Affairs. We have worked with SILT (Sustainable Iowa Land Trust) and Writing the Land in New York. We have contacts and have worked with staff at the Liberty Hyde Bailey Museum in Michigan and the Climate Museum in NYC. I am an emerita ISU Distinguished Professor, a well-published, award-winning writer, with nine books from major publishers. I've toured plays across the country and abroad. I have dual citizenship with the U.S. and Ireland, opening connections to the artistic community throughout the world. www.maryswander.com.

Diversity Initiatives:
AgArts seeks diverse staffing and participation in all its programming. We have highlighted people of difference on our staff and in our podcasts, and seek diverse artists and farmers for our residencies. Through help from the Cynipid Fund, we are working nationally and internationally to continue these efforts. Currently, we are working with the Meskwaki Settlement on a chicken dance for the dedication of a new farm for the Iowa Prairie Center, an urban farm residency, and the hosting of more international artists-in-residence.

The AgArts executive director is disabled and the studio is fully accessible to people with disabilities. We are transcribing many of our podcasts and hope to post this printed material on our website to connect with the deaf community.

Long-Range Goals:
In the future, we hope to raise more funding to increase staffing. New staff members will help to extend the range of our residencies and increase the listenership of our podcasts. We hope to do more work with diversity, increasing residencies for both international artists and people of difference. We hope to grow our podcast listenership to wider, English-speaking communities throughout the world.

In addition to living among the Amish in Iowa and the Hispanic community in New Mexico, I have done major projects with both the blind and deaf communities, with immigrants and with the Meskwaki Settlement. I have taught poetry in inner-city schools. I have had a study abroad course in creative writing, teaching in the schools in Trinidad and Tobago. I would like to brainstorm with some of my contacts in these communities to involve them in increasing diversity in AgArts.

The online memoir class has been especially successful. At this point, two students have received book contracts. I would like to transform this class material into a series of lectures that would be available on the website for a fee to generate a passive stream of income.

We hope to develop the *Blazing Star Journal* presence in the small magazine community with annual awards, key interviews, and the publication of dynamic writing that blends the topics of arts and agriculture.

Support:
AgArts has received grants from the Iowa Arts Council, the Cynipid Fund, the Werner-Ellithorp Fund at the Oregon Community Foundation, and the Kallio-Levine Fund. In addition, we've raised money with Facebook fundraisers and an annual private donor campaign. Any additional support is welcome to help us meet our goals in this exciting and expanding non-profit. Donations can be made through the website at www.agarts.org.

Photo: Wildflowers by Mary Swander

THE MILK HOUSE RURAL WRITING COLLECTIVE

Ireland

The Milk House
rural writing collective

The Milk House works to build a community between those who write about rural subjects and those who want to read about them. We believe that rural life is both singular and unique across geography, while at the same time having aspects that are shared among those who experience it, regardless of where they come from. It means something to be a part of a rural environment, and we want to facilitate those who explore that implication.

We stand behind the power of the story and believe that to share one's experience is both an act of love and an act of resistance. Only when we take the time to examine what is at stake in being human can we all be human together. To do that, we offer a space where short stories, essays, poems and music can meet to communicate the rural life.

Essayist and Photographer:
-Ryan Dennis

Photos by Ryan Dennis
Above: Derrick Dennis (Ryan's Father) Reading
Next Page: Derrick Dennis Working
Page 249: Ryan Dennis Reading
Page 250: Cow
Page 251: Ryan's Aunt and Cousin, Kelly and Jade Atherton
Page 252: Calf

The Stories We Tell
by Ryan Dennis

Some evenings we sat on the front porch and watched the cattle graze on the side hill. My father might comment on the day or the work we had done, but if we stayed on the porch long enough and if he had a glass of gin in his hand, he might tell another story. He would start in with "Did I tell you about the time that…" Usually he already did and we all knew it, but we let recall again a runaway silage wagon and or getting the tractor so buried in mud that they had to hire a backhoe to dig it out.

After recounting these memories he sometimes grew quiet while they replayed in his mind. The cattle in front of us spread through the pasture, flicking their switches at the flies. They would pull at the grass a few times and lift their heads to chew, and then take a few steps and do it again. The sun turned to deeper hues as it headed towards the hill line. At such times I thought we were sitting in stillness, except for the mastication of cattle. It wasn't until I lived away from home for the first time that I realized that what we thought was silence was instead filled with the clatter of birds.

The farm I grew up on was in a rural valley in Western New York that was covered in trees. Once the first light of the morning reached over the horizon the lawn exploded in birdsong. The old walnut trees in the lawn and the hedgerows and nearby gully were heavy with the sounds of sparrows, wrens, other songbirds and sometimes flocks of starlings that blacked out the sky when they lifted into flight. Communing with birds was a natural part of fieldwork. When I plowed, crows followed after me in bunches to pick at the overturned dirt. If I cut hay on a day when the air was heavy I could turn around and watch the barn swallows pick insects out of the air. At any time in an uncut field there may be three or four redwing blackbirds turning in tight circles above the grass. Some birds I recognized in certain fields year after year and nowhere else, and thought I must be privileged to see them.

Our family were dairy farmers during a time that the industry had seen a lot of change. Most family farms like us went out of business, while a few remaining operations grew bigger. My grandfather sold his half of the land to one of the large farms. The first thing they did was rent a bulldozer to take out hedgerows and ditches to gain a few more planting acres. However, those ditches and hedgerows had been there for a long time and served a purpose. Immediately topsoil was lost in the spring runoff. Wet spots grew larger. I wondered for the birds that used those hedgerows. However, the owner of that farm doesn't live nearby and have to drive by those fields every day. Nor do they do fieldwork themselves and watch the birds there.

The expression "ties to the land" always bothered me when I was young. It felt too urban, maybe because it wasn't something we tended to say ourselves. However, since then I've lived in various rural and urban environments, and I haven't come up with anything better. Since my childhood, the way we thought about farming has changed. Back then, it seemed like the world was divided into those who farmed and those who didn't, and we thought all problems, misunderstanding and injustice came from the latter. Now it is different. Today there are small farmers and large farmers, and the type of agriculture between the two are not the same. One of those differences, perhaps, is what it means to have ties to the land.

My father and I spent a lot of time riding in the tractor cab together. When I was small I would wander to whatever field he was working and waited for him to reach the headlands again. The door would swing open and I'd climb up the steps. At twelve I started learning how to do fieldwork myself, beginning with disking or hauling round bales, and then working towards being able to plant corn or chop silage. To teach me, my father would take the tractor and whatever equipment was behind it and go the length of the field and back, and then shove over in the seat and allow me to do it myself. That was how I was taught to run machinery: shown once, and then told of the types of mistakes I could make.

I was nervous, trying to keep the tractor tires straight and avoid the woodchuck holes, but my father pretended not to notice if I let off the clutch a little hard or hit a stone. He'd lean the side of his head against the tractor window and stare through the dusty windshield, probably seeing things that I couldn't. Eventually he would have a story. Maybe it was where he shot his first buck, or why we called the field the name that we did. It could have been about getting stuck or the baler catching fire. It could have been a story he heard from my grandfather, such as when my grandfather plowed with horses at the age of ten and the horse got spooked, broke the harness, and ran into the next town. What my father told me depended on the field we were in, and I'd probably hear it again the next time we were there.

In moments like that it was clear why family farming was a lifestyle and not just a business. The stories, memories and familial history we had with the ground beneath us came from what he did, and it became a part of who we were. We had a personal relationship with the land. The stories we told helped make that relationship something we understood. When someone's identity is attached to a certain piece of land they behave towards that land differently. Our family remained farming long after it was profitable, or logical, to do so. We had invested ourselves on a parcel of hill ground and it was hard for us to imagine ourselves not working it. We considered it home and treated it as such. Some fields were in odd shapes because of diversion ditches, but we kept them that way because it was better for soil conservation. We had no interest in fracking. We rotated crops the best we could. Instead, the factory farm rolls onto my grandfather's field once every few months in a parade of large equipment, compacting the soil more than is healthy for it. They aren't there long enough to make any stories from their experience there. They probably don't notice the birds.

My father has since passed, but there are still others like him who have stories to tell. That was the reason why I started The Milk House, a rural writing collective. Rural life is singular and unique across geography, while at the same time having aspects that are shared among those who experience it, regardless of where they come from. Every week a new story, essay, poem or song is shared that explores the rural experience. Some pieces are from authors who have won major prizes like the National Book Award, and some are from individuals putting pen to paper for the first time. With this impetus, an online community has evolved between those who write on rural subjects and those who want to read about them.

There's something implicit in the work shared on The Milk House, and that's what is at stake if these stories never get to be told. Farming can be an isolating venture—as can other occupations in the countryside, and it becomes even lonelier when the farmer or rural inhabitant can't see their experience reflected back to them in the things they read or watch. Additionally, without sharing these narratives the general public becomes further disconnected from what these people do, and understands less where their food comes from, why it is important to support small agriculture, and why land conservation is necessary. The cultural loss that comes from stories never being shared soon has tangible consequences, especially in shrinking energy and support behind beneficial land management.

Large scale farming, like the kind now done on what used to be our
land, is based on quantitative measurements. Through economies of
scale, these farms gain a financial advantage by growing larger and larger.
The case for small agriculture and land conservation is a different type
of argument, however. It is based on environmental concerns and long
term benefits to rural communities. It speaks to the social capital behind
a better way of treating land, animals and the people between them,
and what is important to us as a society. Sometimes it's hard to find easy
numbers to support that claim. However, just as it is the tales, myths and
personal chronicles that connect the land and the people who work it, so
is it the stories that make up this argument. When we tell stories from a
rural life we're affirming to each other who we are and where our values
lie. We're making sense of what we do in a way that is more meaningful
than the milk, beef or crops that is produced. In the end, that is the
power of the arts: to do the type of work that is hard to measure in yield
statistics.

MARTIN BRIDGE

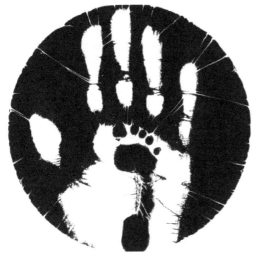

Massachusetts

Handprint by Martin Bridge
www.thebridgebrothers.com

-Essay and Art by Martin Bridge

Mycelial Messanger (Paul Stamets) by Martin Bridge

Handprint, a Journey by Martin Bridge

Being raised by a family of artists, teachers and nature lovers, I have been utterly entranced by the natural world since my childhood. As I grew and became more aware of the many factors that threaten the beauty of life on this planet, I became increasingly concerned about the trajectory of our ever expanding population and an economy that aims for exponential growth while drawing on finite resources.

I realize my worldview is miniscule when compared to the grand scheme, but I see enough on a local scale to feel compelled to take action. While investigating various aspects of the "sustainability" movement, I felt overwhelmed with the multitude of viewpoints one might look at and the numerous pathways one might start to traverse. In addition, I felt what many do, that I didn't have the skills, time or resources to be a part of the solution.

I was never sure of what part I might play in this effort, and then a walk in the woods 15 years ago drastically changed the trajectory of my art, teaching and life as I was introduced to both the Permaculture Concept and the revolutionary work of Mycologist Paul Stamets.

As a friend and I were beginning our wandering through the forest he apologized to me saying that he had meant to bring me a gift of mushroom spawn. At the time I had no idea what that meant and he explained that it was woodships inoculated with mushroom mycelium that you could mix into more wood chips to then create a mushroom bed that would yield gourmet and medicinal mushrooms. I immediately asked if I could cycle my carving waste into this to then eat a part of something that was part of my art, to have it become part of me in a way. As odd as this might sound I was transfixed by this idea and it was that hook that caught my attention enough to drive me to order "Mycelium Running" by Stamets. After reading his work I was hooked (or "Bemushroomed" as many Mycophiles refer to it as). Later in the walk I was introduced to my first Wildcrafted Mushroom. Turkey Tail, Coriolis or Trametes Versicolor is an incredibly common and yet incredibly potent medicinal mushroom that soon became the inspiration for one of my earlier mushroom paintings. Years later it became part of the collection of Paul Stamets himself.

Trametes Versicolor by Martin Bridge

At the same time I ordered "Mycelium Running" I chose to pick up David Holmgren's text "Permaculture, Principles and Pathways Beyond Sustainability". As I worked through that book where chapters were dedicated to illustrating the three core Ethics of Permaculture Design and the 12 Principles that guide design and decision making, I began a series of paintings that were a form of Visual Meditation where I spent time contemplating how I might integrate those ideas and practices into my own work and way of being. Each painting was based on the Icon that was associated with its principle and forced me to move through the text more slowly so that I could digest more of the material instead of just passing through the words as quickly as possible.

If you have heard the term Permaculture and yet have no idea what it is, the meaning of the word may be elusive as so many people use it in different contexts. It is a concept that the visionary Bill Mollison shaped with the help of his former student turned colleague David Holmgren. The Permaculture framework and movement began as a response to Mollison identifying modern industrial agriculture as the single most destructive force on the planet. This concept is challenging for many, as most of us look at agriculture as a way that humankind interacts with nature to provide and fulfill the mission to be fruitful and multiply. I will be honest that as I sit and write this now, it is hard to avoid diverting into a long rant about how destructive the system is, but instead share the astute description of Permaculture teacher Toby Hemenway who describes agriculture (the tending of land,) as a way of "transforming ecosystems into humans".

Mollison and Holmgren sought to revise the system of agriculture, but as they explored altering the techniques of food production it became evident that many related systems had to change along with it. Location, distribution, access, and economics became prominent factors that required addressing as the concept expanded and solidified. The most succinct definition that I like to use is that Permaculture is "A Design Science based on observation of natural systems, to guide the creation of sustainable agricultural, architectural and social systems."

One might also describe Permaculture as meeting the essential needs of a population while utilizing the local resources. For example, growing food organically and locally has been a major component in the way I practice Permaculture. For years this was my personal practice, but as I proceeded further along my learning path, my focus shifted to communication. Prioritizing outreach and education about the success of the Permaculture Movement and acknowledging this shift can only be achieved with an army of practitioners behind it. For years I have been trying to make art that both provides engaging teaching tools, also catches the interest of my audience and then serves as an entry point to important conversations. Through this practice I have found pathways into discussions that have changed peoples lives.

The onset of the Covid 19 Pandemic afforded an interesting opportunity to engage with people who were looking for solutions as we, in some of the most developed countries in the world, saw our healthcare system utterly overwhelmed, and as we watched food, toilet paper and bullets disappear off the shelves with astonishing speed. Suddenly, I found myself with an audience looking for tools to take some small measure of control in their needs for food and medicines. I was simultaneously exploring digital platforms to begin teaching remotely as a part of my professional life as a public school educator, and these became pivotal in guiding a group that swelled to 250 in an exploration of the foundation of ethics, principles and practices of Permaculture. As I spoke to an audience that quite literally was semi-captive in the late winter and into the spring and summer, many of this group began gardens for the first time and found our collective work an effective way to transform anxiety into action. It was a powerful experience to share at that time.

Now, over two years later, many have continued the work that was set in motion during that time. Many have relaxed and returned to the way of being before the pandemic as we "reopened". There is part of me that has been watching the return to the old norm and sadly feel there was an opportunity lost.

(opposite) Time Scout (Bill Mollison) by Martin Bridge

While fear is a potent motivator, it is only so for a time. Our systems can only operate for so long with that as a driving force. Economics can also be a powerful force of change. If unsustainable practices become unaffordable, many will be forced to move away from them.

Both these are negative forces that can wreak havoc on our psyches.

Principal VI Create No Waste by Martin Bridge

If the goal of the Sustainability movement is to nurture a healthier environment for life (to continue) to thrive we must include our minds and spirits and tending to them as a part of our design goals.

Intention is key, and in some ways the word Sustainable has a slight negative connotation especially when we look at where we are. Sustain suggests keeping things "as is." Many are replacing that word with "Regenerative" which holds the possibility that our environment could become more fertile, more productive, more diverse.

After allowing for the possibility that things can improve, we need to find beauty and joy in the practices we engage in. This is easy to find when one wakes up on a pleasant day and steps right outside their doorstep to pick the fresh herbs they will use for their morning tea, or instead of deciding what to have for dinner and then getting in a car to go walk through the aisles of their grocery store to then wait in line before getting back in the car to return home and then begin to prepare the meal to simply walk out one's door and pick whatever is ready for harvest and start there.

These are some things that are easily evident to those that visit my homestead but there is an ethereal dimension that I find harder to display and describe. To me there is certainly a deep spiritual relationship with the land I live on and interact with that is far more *natural* then journeying to a structure to worship the source of life. To me the act of kneeling on the ground is incredibly potent. Here I interact with the soil that contains an incredible complexity of life, and which will in turn nurture and sustain my own life

In addition to composting all the material I can, I return what I can of my form to the soil for a multitude of practical reasons from repelling competing animals to nutrients for the soil as well as more symbolic functions of linking myself with the land that my body is being built from. As I see myself more and more in the land, the care for it becomes increasingly selfish as there is no separation between it's health and mine.

Seeing this in the microcosm of my own small garden and then looking at how it is touched and affected by systems that spread further and further out connecting it to the totality of our biosphere can be quite literally awe inspiring. Looking back and forth between the micro and macro we can see how small actions affect the whole and can have potent effects.

It's easy to see a home-scale garden as a lot of time and energy that may only generate a portion of the food one needs to survive, or we can look at the things that would have gone into generating that same food that may have used synthetic fertilizers and pesticides before getting transported thousands of miles and the subsequent detrimental effects avoided. Then we can see our neighbor doing the same and see the compounding positive effect as more and more small actions leading to a monumental shift for the better.

As I think about my journey and trying to figure out right action and the relationship between my art, teaching, and permaculture efforts, I have often come back to—and found a center point— in the worlds of Permaculture Elder Larry Santoyo who said (in reference to the question of what is the *right* use of energy and resources) "Don't worry… just make sure your Handprint exceeds your Footprint"

SEEDS OF SOLIDARITY

Massachusetts

Seeds of Solidarity consists of a family farm and community based organization. The solar-powered farm uses agroecological methods to regenerate soil and restore climate while growing abundant and nourishing food.

The mission of the organization is to innovate programs that awaken the power among people of all ages–from toddlers to teens to people who are incarcerated– to Grow Food Everywhere to transform hunger to health, and create resilient lives and communities.

In 1998, a conversation among the Seeds of Solidarity founders and neighbors planted the seeds of an idea—to create a festival that would unite residents of their region whose livelihoods are connected to the land and the arts, celebrate a rural low-wealth region that is often over looked, and bring much needed revitalization to their community.

The North Quabbin Garlic and Arts Festival, strongly rooted in grassroots values, remains a neighborhood created and scent-sational success.

-Essay and Photos by Dr. Deb Habib

Peace, Love, and Garlic: How a Neighborhood Ignited Local Culture and Economy
by Deb Habib, EdD

The sun had been up for several hours when my husband Ricky rolled out of bed on an autumn Sunday morning in 1999, the day after our first North Quabbin Garlic and Arts Festival. Sleeping in was uncharacteristic for him as a farmer, along with the fact that he'd had a few beers the night before to celebrate the success of an event created on a wing and a prayer. Ricky had not in fact drank much of any alcohol in the previous decade and his hangover was compounded by little sleep or food in the forty-eight hours prior, which were instead filled with bagging and labeling garlic. The bed from which he rolled was in our tiny hand-built, off the grid cottage, complete with infant drool as his wake up alarm. We were nonetheless ecstatic, because almost a thousand people had found their way to a field in the woods ringed with a dozen hearty artists and farmers, a makeshift music stage, horse-drawn hayride, and one food truck stuck in the mud. They had readily bought the garlic grown with our soil and toil and put a few bucks in the festival donation jar. Their showing up marked the first grassroots event in our low-income, rural community that supported artists and farmers—financially and through the clear message that these livelihoods were valued and vital.

We were new to the North Quabbin region, arriving on a quest for land just outside the unaffordable Connecticut River Valley. In Orange, an old mill town on the eastern edge of Franklin County, we walked overgrown stony fields and forest that did not at all resemble typical farmland and purchased it through a local land trust. We put our no-till methods, farming background, and dedication to work to build soil, start our vegetable and garlic farm, Seeds of Solidarity, and build a home and life for our family.

The festival idea was birthed on a late summer day during our first season on the land. Our neighbor Jim, a native of the region and phenomenal woodworker stopped in. Chatting while Ricky bagged up our gorgeous crop of our garlic, they sharing a similar lament. Where would we sell our beautiful garlic without traveling and taking a wholesale price-cut? Where could Jim show his stunning work that combined fine woodworking with items salvaged from local factories? All of the talented artists and hardworking farmers in our region had to leave town just to find a venue to sell their wares. This spontaneous conversation led to a creative and fateful potluck gathering of five- me and Ricky, Jim and his wife Alyssa and neighbor and potter Lydia Grey. It was 1998 and the 'buy local' craze was in its infancy. It had not yet hit our towns and likely never would in the way the nearby 5-college area would benefit from the buzz. There was beauty and ample skill to be found in our region and it deserved celebrating. After dinner and with ideas flowing, we each dug into our pockets to produce a twenty-dollar bill, creating a crumpled pile of 100 bucks on the center of the table. We met every month, always over shared food, to plan an event that would, according to our mission statement: "Unite North Quabbin people whose livelihoods are connected to the land and the arts, and to invite both local residents and those who do not live in the region to experience the richness of an area that is often overlooked."

We used the $100 bucks to print up postcards to distribute in our local towns. The week before that first festival, a hurricane came through. Neighbors showed up with tractors and gravel to prepare for whatever crowds might show up to a muddy field in the middle of the woods. And they did, almost 1,000 strong.

By the second year of the festival, it was clear we needed a larger space than a clearing in the woods at our place, Seeds of Solidarity Farm. We moved it a mile down the road to spacious Forsters Farm, where Dory Forster welcomed it, honoring her parents who always wanted their former dairy farm to be a gathering place. Her mother Gigi lived into her 90s to see it happen, and to have it grow to 10,000 folks gathering over a weekend in vibrant celebration.

Boston-centric media has portrayed the demoralizing statistics about the North Quabbin as downtrodden and rife with social ills, yet it was immediately apparent even from our short time living there how ripe a region it was, especially in regards to folks who knew how to work with their hands. Until the 1930s an 18-mile long, 5-mile wide Swift River ran through the valley it created, original lands of the Nipmuc people. For years it was rich with rural life, vegetable production, orchards and livestock. In 1938, this valley, with its four communities and the most fertile agricultural land in the area was flooded to create the Quabbin Reservoir in order to supply Boston, 80 miles east, with drinking water. While the creation of the Quabbin enhanced the area's forestry activities and wildlife population, it eradicated most of the agricultural food production potential of the region, placing 38 square miles of our best soil under water. Subsequently, mills and tool companies in the regions two main towns, Orange and Athol, supported the local economies through the 1960s. Then these mills started to close and the vibrancy of the region radically diminished, leaving economic despair in its place. In addition to food insecurity and a population that suffers disproportionately from physical and mental health challenges, high unemployment and foreclosure, there is a prevailing sense of isolation and disenfranchisement among many residents. Although the demographics of the area accurately depict a community in significant stress, the North Quabbin is remarkable in the extent to which people come together in their efforts to improve life in the region. Amidst all of the challenges, there is natural, forested beauty, tremendous community perseverance, and enduring partnerships in our region, and receptivity among the residents to initiatives that bring joy and vitality to our community.

Photo: Portal to the Future: Local Living and Renewable Energy Area
at the North Quabbin Garlic and Arts Festival

Over the years, the North Quabbin Garlic and Arts Festival organizing
committee grew from 5 to 25, all creative and outside of the box
thinkers. Together we've crafted music and performance stages of
lumber from local mills, as well as the long tables at which attendees sit
to sample glorious garlic cuisine from area food vendors. The festival
remains fully volunteer organized, people powered, not profit driven.
There is no president, paid staff, or corporate sponsorship. One unique
organizing element involves each of 100 exhibitors participating in a
festival set-up day or making a hearty meal for these exhibitor/workers.
We implemented this participation model as a way to keep vendor fees
modest while garnering much needed help when the committee was
facing burnout some years back. Moving beyond "show up and sell"
results in fruitful connections among exhibitors and strengthens the
festival as a village, not solely an event. Many of our exhibitors got
their food or art business start at the festival! The weekend of, 150
more volunteers park cars, welcome attendees, work recycle/compost
stations, or deliver treats from our wood fired oven to other volunteers.
Environmental values are at the heart of the festival, with one astounding
example being only 2 bags of trash produced for close to ten thousand
people, with everything else recycled or transformed into rich compost
for local gardens.

Collaboration combined with a just do it attitude are core to the event's sustained success and the positive vibe that permeates. Attendees feel good when they step onto the foliage ringed festival fields, and usually better when they leave. We've never done a business plan or feasibility study, which we joke would have come out as...a joke. It would not likely have projected that thousands of people would show up on an isolated field in one of the lowest wealth communities in the state. Ingenuity, muscle, and magical thinking have reigned. In the early days, we had to call repeatedly to convince the then editor of an arts and culture paper centered in the adjacent and more affluent college town region to list the festival in their calendar section. They proclaimed that "no one wanted to go to Orange." We countered that he was wrong and red-lining our community. And he was, in fact, wrong.

Above: Garden of Peace and Non-Violence installation created at the festival field; Opposite: Garlic Harvest at Seeds of Solidarity Farm (some of 15,000 bulbs)

Fast forward to a winter afternoon, January 2022. The committee is gathered around a firepit, tea mugs in mitten clad hands, happy to not be zooming as we affirm the post Covid-19 return of the 24th Annual North Quabbin Garlic and Arts Festival. During the pandemic hiatus, the committee kept up the festival spirit and our connection. We held a virtual festival, offered a free marketplace for artists struggling for sales, and dug into reserves to make small grants as we'd done each year, giving $10,000 to a dozen local causes even without any festival income. (We've donated 50,000 total to a range of small local arts, social justice, wellness, and environmental groups). Tradition is to start each monthly meeting or pre-festival workday meal with a gently revealing question that builds appreciation of each other. Values have always been at the heart of Garlic and Arts, so sharing some in the cold fresh air provided a ceremonial restart moment. Connection, healing from isolation, relearning, staying joyful, support for artist/farmer livelihoods were voiced among many reasons to bring the festival back.

After a few more winter meetings around a fire, on an April Sunday we gathered at the festival site to clear two years of fallen branches, and sweep the dust and debris from the stage we'd built together of local lumber. We needed a break, and unfortunately it came in the form of a Covid-19 hiatus. But the excitement to bring back this celebration was and is palpable, one long infused with cooperation, self-determination, and a belief that together we can and must envision and shape the communities in which we want to live.

SERPENTINE ART AND NATURE COMMONS

New York

Where in New York City can you hike hilly trails through beautiful native trees and plants, see rare geological sites, and observe hawks, owls, raccoons, and opossums all while enjoying spectacular views of New York Harbor, Brooklyn and Queens, the New Jersey Highlands, and the Verrazano Bridge? At the Serpentine Art and Nature Commons on the North Shore of Staten Island.

The Serpentine Art and Nature Commons (SANC) is a not-for-profit community based group founded in 1978 and dedicated to the preservation and maintenance of woods and hillside on the east shore of Staten Island.

Our nature preserve provides open space and educational opportunities to some of the most crowded neighborhoods on Staten Island. SANC is open to the entire community. We encourage tax-deducatable membership, our major source of income.

-Poet Maria Perez

Serpentine Art and Nature Commons

In the 19th century the industrial village of Stapleton developed at the bottom of Grymes Hill. Several of its breweries drilled caves into the hillside to store beer. Wealthy families built fanciful Victorian mansions at the top of the hill. For the most part, the land on the hillside itself was left undisturbed - primarily because the severity of the slope discouraged builders. In the 1960's a planned development on the steepest part of the hill was successfully opposed by concerned neighbors, but not before 3 acres of topsoil had been removed.

Ownership of 11 ½ acres of the hillside was assumed by the Trust for Public Land (TPL). They encouraged concerned neighbors to form Serpentine Art and Nature Commons (SANC) to maintain and improve the land as a nature preserve open to the community.

SANC's first tasks were to clean up our wooded lands and begin the long process of rebuilding our denuded land. We removed trash, removed almost 100 abandoned cars, and installed fencing to prevent further dumping. The lower, flat land was made into a small neighborhood park with flowers, trees, and art exhibits. Trails through the woods and a scenic overlook at the top of the hill were completed. Neighborhood youth and a part-time groundskeeper were hired to maintain the grounds. SANC offered its expertise to other groups devoted to preserving hillside land.

SANC's hillside is the result of glacial movement and continental collisions and includes a variety of geological formations. Most notable is the serpentine barren. This is olive green scaly rock that crumbles easily. It is rare in the New York area and supports a unique variety of plant life.

SANC maintains several trails on its property. These trails provide access to the wooded areas, serpentine barrens, and a scenic promenade. One trail starts from our main entrance on Van Duzer St. and climbs steeply to an intersection about two-thirds of the way up the hill. There the trail splits. The trail to the left goes through wooded lands and past a glacial sinkhole ultimately climbing via a step staircase to Howard Ave. It also connects to another trail (not on SANC land) which runs through to Park Lane The trail to the right climbs an additional 100 feet to a scenic overlook and serpentine barren and then loops around to join the trail to the left. A map of the trails is at the Van Duzer Street entrance.

Our scenic overlook faces lower New York Harbor and provides vistas from the New Jersey Highlands to Far Rockaway. It is an excellent place to view the Verrazano Bridge, Coney Island, and the variety of ships in the harbor.

Serpentine Arts

Created by Eric Alter the Artist

SERPENTINE ART & NATURE COMMONS, INC.
Presents

The Ground We Share: Land Art Sculptures of Serpentine Commons

Featuring the art of Eric Alter and members of the Wooley Collective: Douglas Schwartz, Rachel Therres and Steve Soloway.

Saturday, September 10, 2016
10:00 AM to 5:30PM

Rain Date Saturday, September 17

Sponsored (in part) by a DCA Premier Grant from Staten Island Arts, with public funding from New York City Department of Cultural Affairs.

String Creations by Eric Alter the Artist

Blue Pill
by Maria Perez

In this forest
I find peace in the destruction of the world I
used to believe was everlasting
I used to let myself fall apart to keep my
memories be the last one standing
I woke up and saw everything I loved became
too demanding
They were stripped away the moment I saw
their true demons
Those demons were named expectations, an
infestation to the notion of my loves sensation
The grass I lay in bites into my flesh as I lose
track of the seasons
These thoughts fill my throat and spill
What a shame, that it can only be numbed by a small blue pill
The black gust of wind somehow puts my heart at ease
I feel a relief in the way time is frozen, as I breathe what seems to be my
last breath
It takes the bliss of collateral damage to realize I have always been
broken

As We Walk
by Maria Perez

The ghost of my memories watches and stands still
As I walk up this empty hill
With native trees, plants, and bare serpentine rock
The light waves of calamity within the pool of grimy water that sits
nearby
It's eyes deep below watches closely, twisting my words into every lie I've
ever told so grossly
They judge me, while I am a continuous redefining mess
Trying to confine a soul like mine to fit in
As I'm walking deeper I taste the poison, I try to close my mouth but my
heart is left open
Like the poison ivy I try so hard to avoid, it stings my body until I dig
holes into my skin to finally free every sin I ever managed to hold inside
my bones
All I wanted was to be known, yet I was never meant to feel their love, I
was meant to feel my own
I question who I am because their expectations are the very bane of my
existence
I walk further up the hill in hopes that with every step I take, and every
bruise that touches my legs, my attempts at earning love serves some
kind of purpose
Thorns prick my veins as I step into this rose bush that's missing all the
roses
As they peel away this god forsaken vessel, I hope they remember we
bleed the same
For now I know that my significance has always been hidden in my name

SANC is notable for its variety of ecosystems including wooded hillsides, glacial sinkholes, and bare serpentine rock. Most of its land remains in a natural state and is covered with native trees and plants. They are a good example of the natural cycle of growth, maturity, and decline.

Opossums, raccoons, squirrels, rabbits, and a variety of birds live in its underbrush and trees. A colony of red tailed hawks has developed and can often be seen floating above our woods. Land stripped of topsoil is going through a natural redevelopment and reflects the tenacity of plant life in a hostile environment.

The Realization
by Maria Perez

The trees within our heart, as it beats throughout the
branches and the leaves
planting seed after seed inside my vessel, wondering if time will be
helpful
Time seems to be friends with the Devil
For I never liked to chase after something I couldn't hold onto
Your scent sets a wildfire to my lungs, it keeps the core of my body warm
on the coldest of days, when I am too tired to spark my own flame
A fire so strong the smoke will fill my throat so that I always remember
your name and how we became,
So that you remain in my bones
Take my lungs apart and fill it with vines so that
everytime I breathe I am reminded of your
presence, a foundation of love it's as strong
as stone, every piece filled with essence

Time is holding hands with the devil, in it's control, it will never be mine
Paralyzed from the bite of Satan's serpentine
There's a fault in our scars
Where thorns grow and make it their home
Yet it took time to realize the way flowers bloomed was the doing of my
own
When the luminous creations of this forest starts to turn gray
I look around and do everything to keep the soil alive and it's peace
protected
But I still fight not to win but to survive, even when it's been infected

I'll trace every memory with my fingertips and bring it back to life
Even when the poison from the polluted air drips onto the ground and
brings strife
When there's whispers from below, "what is the point of anything when
the home you tried so hard to protect, no longer has the strength to
stand"
As my home turns to shambles, I'll say "there is a point in everything, my
soul will still remain in this land".

☼

Poets' Biographies

Amy M. Alvarez is a Black Latina poet and educator. She has been awarded fellowships from CantoMundo, VONA, Macondo, VCCA, and the Furious Flower Poetry Center. Her poetry has appeared or is forthcoming in *Ploughshares, New Ohio Review, River Styx, Colorado Review, Crazyhorse, Alaska Quarterly Review,* and elsewhere. Born in New York City to Jamaican and Puerto Rican parents, she now lives and teaches in Morgantown, West Virginia.

Willeena Booker is an elementary school teacher and a poet. She enjoys writing poetry that touches the heart and challenges the mind. Her work has been published by Moonstone Arts Center's *Poetry Ink Anthology 2021, Haiku 2021, 2022 Anthology,* and *NonSense Verse Anthology* 2021. Poet Project has featured her poem *I Matter* on their BIPOC poetry page and she was a finalist for the *Rise Up* Anthology by *Oprell Magazine.* She lives in Pennsylvania with her husband and daughters.

Paul Brooke has five full-length collections of poetry including *Light and Matter: Poems and Photographs of Iowa* (2008) and *Meditations on Egrets: Poems and Photographs of Sanibel Island* (2010), *Sirens and Seriemas: Photographs and Poems of the Amazon and Pantanal* (2015), *Arm Wrestling at the Iowa State Fair* (2018) and *The Skald and the Drukkin Tröllaukin: Photographs and Poems of Iceland* (forthcoming 2022). Dr. Brooke is a Professor of English at Grand View University in Des Moines, Iowa.

Catalina Marie Cantú (Xicana) is a multi-genre writer, Jack Straw Fellow, Alum of VONA, and The Mineral School. She has received funding from Artists' Trust, Hugo House, Centrum, and Hedgebrook. Her poems and stories have been published and anthologized. Cantú earned a B.A. in La Raza Studies, and a J.D. from the University of Washington. She is Board member of the UNESCO Seattle City of Lit, Board President of La Sala Latinx Artists', and lives in West Seattle.

Scott Chaskey is a poet, farmer, and educator. For 30 years he cultivated crops and community at Quail Hill Farm, Amagansett, N.Y., one of the original CSA's in the country. He has served as a founding Board member for three not-for-profits focused on land equity and social justice, and he has traveled widely as a writer and speaker. Author of *This Common*

Ground (Viking), *Seedtime* (Rodale), *Stars are Suns* (poetry), his work-in-progress, *Soil and Spirit*, will be published by Milkweed Editions in 2022.

John L. Dutton II has over twenty years of teaching experience, the last fifteen of which he has taught language arts at the middle school level. Since 2013, John has actively been involved with two writing groups, Write by the Rails (WbtR) and the Prince William Poet Laureate Circle. He is a life member of the Virginia Writers' Club and the Poetry Society of Virginia. In 2015, he created Spilled Ink, an open-mic night that meets on the fourth Friday of every month to celebrate the written word.

Doris Frazier is a Charlotte, North Carolina Native and graduate of Johnson C. Smith University. She had a dedicated career as a teacher and is a life-long respected Church/ Community Artist of Historic Theater groups. She presents Poetry-Performances often using selected poems from her work *Writes for the Young*.

Dianna L. Grayer PhD., is a Marriage and Family Therapist in Northern California and has been in private practice for over 25 years. She is also an author, speaker, playwright, director and producer. She spends most of her free time writing poems, plays and children's books. Dr. Grayer loves to empower, inspire and educate others so that they can live fuller and happier lives.

Duane L. Herrmann's books include *Prairies of Possibilities, Ichnographical: 173, Family Plowing, Remnants of a Life, No Known Address, Praise the King of Glory, Gedichte aus Prairies of Possibilities, Escape From Earth*, and chapbooks. He has been published in anthologies, *Midwest Quarterly, Little Balkans Review, Flint Hills Review, Orison, Inscape, Lily Literary Journal, Hawai'i Review* and others in English and other languages. He received a Robert Hayden Poetry Fellowship, and a Ferguson Kansas History Book Award.

Jillian Hishaw, is an agricultural attorney, founder, and C.E.O. of F.A.R.M.S and Hishaw Law LLC. Inspired by her own family's land loss, this international non-profit provides technical and legal assistance to small farmers, while reducing hunger in the farmer's community. She wrote *Don't Bet the Farm on Medicaid*, and *Systematic Land Theft*. She is published in op-ed articles in *Civil Eats, The Counter, and HempLand U.S.A.*, and featured in *O, The Atlantic*, and *Vice News,* among others.

Rodger Martin's *For All The Tea in Zhōngguó*, 2019, follows *The Battlefield Guide*, and the selection of *The Blue Moon Series* by Small Press Review as one of its bi-monthly picks of the year. He's received an Appalachia award for poetry, NHSCA's award for fiction, fellowships from the NEH His work has appeared in journals and anthologies throughout the United States and China.

Poet, editor, and educator **Dana Maya** is from what Américo Paredes called "Greater Mexico"—a space transcending geopolitical, cultural, linguistic, & creative borders. She was educated at Vassar College & the University of Texas at Austin, with an orientation in Chicanx, Queer, & Race Studies. She's taught literature & writing at colleges, public schools, & community organizations. Her writing has won awards & appears in anthologies, journals, stages, museums, memorials, & other public spaces.

Stephanie Morningstar is Kanien'kehá:ka, Wakeniáhten (Mohawk nation, Turtle clan), with ancestors rooted in Six Nations of the Grand River Territory and Europe. She is a plant nerd, medicine tender, bridge builder, soil and seed steward, scholar, and Earth Worker dedicated to decolonizing and liberating minds, hearts, and land- one plant, person, ecosystem, and non-human being at a time. Stephanie is Co-Director of Northeast Farmers of Color Land Trust and a PhD student.

Antoni Ooto lives and works in rural upstate New York with his wife poet/storyteller, Judy DeCroce. He is an internationally published poet and flash fiction writer. Well-known for his abstract expressionist art, Antoni now adds his voice to poetry. His recent poems have been published in many journals and anthologies. He is a frequent contributor to *Vita Brevis Press*, *The BeZINE*, *Amethyst Review*, *Front Porch Review*, *Ponder Savant*, *The Poet Magazine*, and *The Active Muse*.

Naima Penniman is a devotee of seeds, multidimensional artist, story teller, movement builder, medicine grower, healer, and educator; co-founder of WILDSEED Healing Village, Director of Education at Soul Fire Farm, and healing practitioner at Harriet's Apothecary. Published in *All We Can Save*, *We Are Each Other's Harvest*, *Farming While Black*, *Climbing PoeTree* and *Semillas*, Naima's poetry has inspired thousands of people and movements across the world. naimainfinity.com

Maria Perez is an 18 year old writer, poet, and artist. Diagnosed with manic depression and anxiety as a teen, she is determined to live, having learned balance through painting and writing. She puts the most vulnerable parts of her heart into her work, and aspires to use her voice to inspire others to do the same. Maria attends Kingsborough Community College pursuing her dream of becoming a teacher. Her poem "Sincerely, you" was published in the Young Writers USA *Imagine*.

Suzanne S. Rancourt was born and raised in the mountains of West Central Maine. Her rural, woodland upbringing offered her the experiential framework that she now uses working with artists/recipients, survivors of Traumatic Brain Injury, other life altering traumatic events, or people living with disability challenges, Ms. Rancourt has further developed her experiences with formal education, military service, and 30+ years of professional practice.

Rita Mae Reese is author of *The Book of Hulga* (2016), which won the Felix Pollak Prize, and *The Alphabet Conspiracy* (2011), which won the 2012 Drake Emerging Writers Award. Her poetry has been nominated for a Pushcart Prize, and her work is featured in *From Where You Dream: The Process of Writing Fiction* (2005) and *Poetry From Sojourner: A Feminist Anthology* (2004). Reese serves as the co-director of literary arts programming at Arts + Literature Laboratory (ALL).

Patti (Spady) Ross graduated from the Ellington School for the Performing Arts, American University and the Keller Graduate School of Management. She holds a certificate in Writing for Social Justice from the University of California, and is published in *The Rural America Newspapers*. She is the spoken word artist "little pi." Her publications include *St. Paul Street Provocations* (Yellow Arrow: 2021), and her poem "Indemnity" was nominated for the 2021 Pushcart Prize. littlepisuniverse.com

Malyk Rowell is a member of The Males Place, and an 8th-grader who is homeschooled in an African-centered environment. He excels in math and science, with a special interest in learning about the universe. His aspirations including electrical engineering and video game design in order to make an impact on his community with fun, engaging, culturally uplifting video games for young black men to play. He wants to strengthen his family and community and make them proud of him.

Leona Sevick is an Asian American poet and the 2017 Press 53 Poetry Award Winner for her book *Lion Brothers*. Her work appears in *Orion, Birmingham Poetry Review,* and *Blackbird,* and *The Golden Shovel Anthology: New Poems Honoring Gwendolyn Brooks*. She is a 2019 Walter E. Dakin Fellow and a 2018 Tennessee Williams Scholar. A poetry reader for *Los Angeles Review,* and advisory board member of the Furious Flower Black Poetry Center, she is professor of English at Bridgewater College.

Laura Shovan is an editor, educator, children's author, and Pushcart Prize nominated poet. Her books include *Mountain, Log, Salt and Stone,* winner of the Harriss Poetry Prize, *Life in Me Like Grass on Fire: Love Poems,* and *Voices Fly* (co-edited with Virginia Crawford). Laura is a longtime poet-in-the-schools. Her award-winning novels for children are *The Last Fifth Grade of Emerson Elementary, Takedown,* and *A Place at the Table,* co-written with Saadia Faruqi.

Julie Sumner is a writer who has worked as a critical care nurse, transplant coordinator, and massage therapist. She recently completed her MFA in poetry at Seattle Pacific University. Her work has appeared in *Wondrous Real, Fathom Magazine, The Cresset, Juxtaprose, San Pedro River Review, Catalpa Magazine,* and *The Behemoth*. She writes and teaches poetry classes in Nashville, Tennessee.

Mary Swander, AgArts executive director and recent Poet Laureate of the State of Iowa, has published over thirteen books of poetry and non-fiction, in addition to plays, radio and television scripts. She has appeared in such places as *The New Yorker, The New York Times Magazine, National Public Radio,* and *Poetry Magazine*. Swander's plays *Map of my Kingdom, Vang* and *Farmscape* have toured the U.S. including a performance at the USDA for the Sec. Tom Vilsack.

Linda Warren lives in Princeton, Massachusetts with her dogs, where she writes, grows vegetables, fishes for trout, and watches birds, rivers, wildlife, stars, and dragonflies.

Rebecca Wee is a professor of English and creative writing at Augustana College in Rock Island, IL. She is the author of *Uncertain Grace,* an award-winning collection of poems published by Copper Canyon Press in 2001 and she has lived in Davenport, IA on the Mississippi since 2003. She grew up in Minnesota, dividing summers between the family cabin on Kabekona Lake and her mother's family ranch in South Dakota. With few exceptions, her poems are full of trees, leaves, weather and stones.

Hyperion Çaca Yvaire (Li/He) is an Atakapa Ishak and Sea Kréyòl territorial practice artist-researcher, a sovereign poet, and kinmaker. His sculptural and sonic work explores the afterlives and aftershocks of collision through investigating administrative, legislative, and wave phenomena. As a territorial researcher, he is interested in the matter resulting from the collision of materials, practices, and claims. @hyperruin

Essayists' and Artists' Biographies

Joanne Alberda has been a resident of Iowa for over 50 years. She spent most of her professional life teaching art at Dordt University and after retirement has devoted her energies to landscape photography and fiber art.

Martin Bridge carries his family tradition forth as he lives, creates and teaches in Western Massachusetts. His work spans a wide range of media: Drawing, Painting, Sculpture, Theater Design, Site Specific Installations, and Performance. As an avid Permaculture designer he strives to improve his awareness of how he relates to the natural world and to live in better balance. Through his work he hopes to inspire and cultivate a greater sense of mystery and possibility.   thebridgebrothers.com

Janine Calsbeek began taking photos when she interned as a journalist at a small town newspaper. Since then, she and her husband Doug have raised two children, she has written and taken photos for many feature stories, she has served as director of Orange City Arts, and she has worked with Mary Swander and AgArts. She enjoys walking, bicycling, gardening, traveling, supporting sustainable agriculture, and sitting in the backyard with a book.

Christopher Canipe is a full-time RVer who wanders North America. When he's not writing software, he's often studying, exploring, and photographing his natural surroundings. You can find Chris' photos on Instagram at @christophercanipe.

Brett Ciccotelli lives on the rocky coast of Maine, close enough to a few small whitewater rivers and tidal waves and bays that his passions for fresh and salt waters are balanced. He's been lucky to have farmed, taught, and traveled across the United States and the world.

Ryan Dennis is the author of the novel *The Beasts They Turned Away* published by époque press, as well as the founder of The Milk House, a rural writing collective. A former Fulbright recipient and PhD in creative writing, his fiction, personal essays and poetry have appeared in numerous literary journals. He has taught creative writing at several universities. Most recently he was a Writer-in-Residence at Maynooth University in Ireland.

Suzan Erem is a founder and the executive director of the Sustainable Iowa Land Trust (SILT). In 2015, she and 24 others launched SILT as a structural solution to saving the family farm in Iowa. SILT takes land off the market in perpetuity for any use but ecologically-based table food production. This reduces or eliminates the land debt built into farming, freeing up resources for a diversity of farmers to experiment with crops and grow food regeneratively.

Marty Espinola became interested in photography at the age of 15 and soon was developing and printing his pictures in a makeshift darkroom. Later as a school teacher he worked weekends as a newspaper and freelance photographer. Now retired, he enjoys pursuing his love of nature photography, mentoring local photography groups and teaching workshops.   lighteffects.shutterfly.com

Dr. Deborah Leta Habib is among the Garlic and Arts Festival founders, and counts the committee members among her favorite people ever. Her day job is running Seeds of Solidarity Farm and Education Center with her beloved co-conspirator, Ricky Baruch. They are authors of *Making Love While Farming: A Field Guide to a Life of Passion and Purpose* (Levellers Press, 2019) which includes many more stories and tools for living on the land and outside the box.

Hiram Larew founded *Poetry X Hunger* in 2018. His most recent collection of poems is *Mud Ajar* (Atmosphere Press, 2021). He lives in Maryland, USA. HiramLarewPoetry.com PoetryXHunger.com

George Leinbaugh settled in Downeast Maine after retiring from the military, and volunteers to conserve the Atlantic Salmon. He is board president of the Downeast Salmon Federation. In his off-time he enjoys fly fishing, kayaking, hunting, and snowshoeing.

JuPong Lin, an immigrant from Taiwan, weaves her ancestral traditions into community performances, cultivating kinship between humans of different places and with our more-than-human kin. As an artist, de/colonial and institutional activist and educator, she fuses story circle, qigong, and cultural somatics in a relational art that bridges personal and collective healing. JuPong currently chairs the MFA in Interdisciplinary Arts program at Goddard College.

Ian McSweeney is Director of Agrarian Trust. His work has focused on the human connection to land, food, and community. He has worked as a social worker; founded a brokerage and consulting company; served as Executive Director of the Russell Foundation; and participated in many farmland and food systems initiatives locally, regionally, and nationally. Ian and his wife Liz and their two boys Dylan and Bridger live on a small farm in southern NH.

Stephanie Morningstar is Kanien'kehá:ka, Wakeniáhten (Mohawk nation, Turtle clan), with ancestors rooted in Six Nations of the Grand River Territory and Europe. She is a plant nerd, medicine tender, bridge builder, soil and seed steward, scholar, and Earth Worker dedicated to decolonizing and liberating minds, hearts, and land- one plant, person, ecosystem, and non-human being at a time. Stephanie is Co-Director of Northeast Farmers of Color Land Trust and a PhD student.

Diane Wilbon Parks is a poet, visual artist and author of two poetry collections and a children's book. A permanent installation of her art and poem is at the Patuxent Research Refuge. Her artwork has been exhibited in local Art Galleries, Libraries, and Online, and featured in *Beyond Words Literary Magazine, 3rd Edition of Ireland's Wexford Women Magazine*, the United Nations Web Page, *Poetry X Hunger*, and the *Voices of Woodlawn*. She created a book cover for *The WriteBlend Poetry Collection*.

A retired professor of literature and writing, **James Calvin Schaap** is the author of numerous books and articles and, most recently, a collection of historical podcasts, "Small Wonders: A Museum of Stories from the Missouri River," originally broadcast on KWIT, NPR affiliate in Sioux City, Iowa. He and his wife have two adult children. They live in Alton, Iowa.

A person of First Nations ancestry, **Tom Speer** carries the Tlawitsis Nation name **lakw'alás** (Place-of-the-Fire). His mother is descended from Princess Angeline and Chief Seattle, the Duwamish & Suquamish

Confederacy leader. Speer is an artist, author, educator, mentor, and Treaty Rights advocate in Chief Seattle City. He served 10 years on Duwamish Tribal Services Board of Directors. He served 5 years as Advisor to the Duwamish Tribal Council.

Haley Stein works in communications and development for Downeast Salmon Federation. A relatively new Mainer, Haley feels at home in scenic, wild Downeast, and loves exploring its dynamic terrain.

Mary Swander, AgArts executive director and recent Poet Laureate of the State of Iowa, has published over thirteen books of poetry and non-fiction, in addition to plays, radio and television scripts. She has appeared in such places as *The New Yorker, The New York Times Magazine, National Public Radio,* and *Poetry Magazine.* Swander's plays *Map of my Kingdom, Vang* and *Farmscape* have toured the U.S. including a performance at the USDA for the Sec. Tom Vilsack.

Judy Thompson finds inspiration exploring the fields, farms and wild places which surround her Iowa home. Her artwork speaks to the complex relationships within our ecosystem and our personal connection to the landscape.   judythompsonwatercolors.com

Noah Wurtz is a writer, gardener, and activist living in Cambridge, Massachusetts. After spending time working on rural and urban farms, Noah dedicated his time to exploring the relationship between land access, climate resilience, and social justice in agriculture. He currently writes for the blog of Agrarian Trust on topics ranging from racism in conservation to pollinator habitats. When not writing, Noah can be found playing fiddle or tending his vegetable garden.

Hyperion Çaca Yvaire (Li/He) is an Atakapa Ishak and Sea Kréyòl territorial practice artist-researcher, a sovereign poet, and kinmaker. His sculptural and sonic work explores the afterlives and aftershocks of collision through investigating administrative, legislative, and wave phenomena. As a territorial researcher, he is interested in the matter resulting from the collision of materials, practices, and claims. @hyperruin

Epilogue
Food has a Way of it's Own

One of the things that has stuck with me from my own study and reflection upon food is that food is a term we use to refer to gifts of the land that are meant to nourish us, sacrifices that the land has made. So that we are made strong. Food is a word that we apply to a series of diverse relationships with land, and relationships in which land is actually very active. Food is a way in which we almost render passive the land and other beings and it's a really terrible thing. But holding on to that knowledge or holding on to that perspective, right now, I want to push past what food is and push past even the idea of food as medicine and really think about foodways and recipes. These recipes are not just spiritual from a cultural perspective, but perhaps that they are actually materially the spirit—the spirits visit us at particular places, and, there's something really potent about recognizing that in your dish, you have a congress of multiple beings that you have to take into your body. And they will do strange things that you will never see, that you cannot visualize. There are other beings in your body, who are going to be nourished by this Congress, by whatever discourse was experienced as you took that bowl to your mouth, there's something awe-inducing about it, that we don't get when we refer to food as a commodity. We have to understand food as having a way of its own.

— Hyperion Çaca Yvaire,
(excerpt of a conversation with JuPong Lin)
August 2022

Photo: Mushrooms by Marty Espinola